施璐德亚洲有限公司 编

施璐德年鉴 2019

VISION DRIVEN LIFE

CNOOD 2008 TO 2019

復旦大學出版社

CNOOD Yearbook (2019)

目录

1
施璐德十年发展纲领
Ten-Year Development Program of CNOOD

15
写在施璐德十周年
On the 10th Anniversary of the Founding of CNOOD
Dennis Chi

24
《共同利益论——基于国际经济视角》新书发布会成功举办
Common Interest Theory — Based on International Economic Perspective Launched in Success

32
没有办不好的事　上下齐心事使成
We'll Make It with One Mind
Heron Tang

35
施璐德数字化升级实践
Digital Upgrading in CNOOD
Ken Xu & Nick Zhang

41
战略伙伴关系
Strategic Partnership
Amir Tafti

51
2019年，我与施璐德不平凡的一年
2019, A Marvelous Year for Me and CNOOD
Wenxin Huang

55
未来·即来
The Future Is Coming
Neo Wu

59
海外施工感触
My Overseas Construction Experiences
Peter Tao & Thompson Lee

68
写给施璐德所有成员的一首诗
A Poem for All CNOOD's Members
Nicolas Kipreos

70
哪些特点成就了别具特色的施璐德
Which Are the Characteristics That Make CNOOD a Unique Company?
Nicolas Kipreos

75
与正能量光芒的人同行
Advancing in the Company of Men with Positive Energy
Tina Jiang

80
回首 2019
Looking Back on 2019
Dorothy Hua

85
成长的意义
The Significance of Growth
Billy Gu

92
光从哪里来
The Source of Light
Jane Yan

102
一缕思绪
A Wisp of Thought
Jeff Xu

108
感恩相遇　不负遇见
Thank Goodness I Have Met You
Heather Zhang

114
心怀光明，向暖而生
With Love in Heart
Danni Xu

119
不一样的春节
An Unusual Spring Festival
Jenna Hu

124
娱乐至死
Amusing Ourselves to Death
Johnson Shen

129
迟来的一封告别信
A Late Farewell Letter
Loreen Luo

147
永远一家人
We Are a Family Forever
Angela Liu

150
念海霞
For Haixia, My Little Sister
Dennis Chi

156
爷 爷
Grandpa
Nancy Qi

158
南楼令·中秋
South Tower Song — Mid-Autumn Festival
Tony Liu

161
实习感悟
My Days as an Intern
Xuzheng Ren

164
实习感想
My Internship
Leo Jiang

166
实习总结
My Internship
Shiying Liu

170
实习总结
My Internship in CNOOD
Jessie Wang

施璐德十年发展纲领

（2020—2029年）

Ten-Year Development Program of CNOOD

(2020 – 2029)

一、序言

在施璐德，最大的自由就是拥有选择的自由——选择个人角色的自由、选择合作团队的自由、选择发展方向的自由、选择业务模式的自由……当然，最重要的自由是选择实现人生价值的自由。

二、愿景

以共同利益论为理论指导，致力于打造一个共创、共治、共享的无边界的有机生态系统，同心协力、众志成城，为把施璐德建成人人爱之、惜之、趋之的梦想之地而努力奋斗。

I. Prologue

At CNOOD, the greatest freedom is the freedom of choice—the freedom in choosing individual roles, cooperative teams, development orientation, business models, etc. Nevertheless, the most important one is the freedom to fulfill the value of our lives.

II. Vision

With the theory of common interests as our guidance, we devote ourselves to creating an organic ecosystem without boundary, which is created, managed and shared by all its members. We will work in full cooperation and with unity of purpose, and strive to build CNOOD into a dreamland which everyone loves, cherishes and gravitates to.

三、战略定位

未来十年，坚持以工程板块为龙头，以工程创造的贸易为基础，以教育为支撑的发展战略；不断积累，兼顾守成，以资源禀赋为引领，以技术为导向，以金融工具为助力，加大创新力度，打造一条员工、公司可持续发展的道路。

III. Strategic Positioning

In the next ten years, we will adhere to our development strategy which, with the engineering segment playing a leading role, is based on engineering-related trade and underpinned by education. We will continue to accumulate while carrying on what has been started. With resource endowment as the driving force, orientated by technologies and boosted by financial instruments, we will intensify innovation and create a path of sustainable development for both the company and its members.

四、十年规划目标

1. 持续拓展全球布局

1.1 加大资本、人员及技术投入，进一步优化资源配置，强化在重点区域的现有业务巩固及新业务开发。以项目机会为契机，进一步完善并推进合伙人、分公司、子公司三级海外业务发展体系建设，推进全球业务布局。

1.2 对合伙人、分公司、子公司建

IV. Objectives of the Ten-Year Program

1. Continuing to extend our global business network

1.1 We will increase our investment of capital, human resources and technology, further optimize the allocation of resources and redouble our efforts to consolidate existing businesses and develop new ones in key regions. We will draw on project opportunities to further improve and promote the building of the three-tier (partner — branch office — subsidiary) overseas business development system, thus strengthening our global business network.

1.2 We will establish assessment and

立考评体系。对所有分公司开展年度考评，利润贡献较大分公司，在下一年度优先考虑升级为子公司。对子公司业务进行双年考评，利润贡献持续增长的子公司，应优先考虑下一年度加大投入。对持续亏损或不赢利的子公司或分公司，应在当期考评结束的下一年，降级或关停。对合伙人实行双年考评，业务突出的合伙人加大对其支持力度。

1.3 在大力推进重点区域业务发展的同时，积极响应国家政策导向，投入更多资源参与"一带一路"沿线国家项目跟踪，并合理策划方案，提高项目落地比例。在条件成熟的"一带一路"沿线国家，优先发展合伙人，建立分公司或子公司。

evaluation systems for partners, branch offices and subsidiaries. For all branch offices, assessments and evaluations will be conducted on an annual basis. Any branch office that has made a relatively big profit contribution will be given priority to be upgraded to a subsidiary in the following year. For subsidiaries, assessments and evaluations will be conducted on a biennial basis. Priority should be given to any subsidiary whose profit contributions have been constantly increasing when we are to increase investment in the following year. Any subsidiary or branch office that has continuously been running at a loss or has failed to make a profit should be downgraded or closed in the subsequent year after the assessment and evaluation. For partners, assessment and evaluation will be conducted on a biennial basis. More support will be provided for partners who have delivered outstanding performance in their business.

1.3 While making great efforts to advance our business in key regions, we actively respond to the government's policies and devote more resources to following the projects located in countries along the Belt and Road. In addition, we will work out rationalized plans to increase the proportion of projects actually implemented. We will give priority to countries with mature conditions along the Belt and Road when we recruit partners or set up overseas branch offices or subsidiaries.

1.4 加强对各国政治风险评估，充分防范法律合规性等风险，及时做出布局调整。在政治稳定、风险较小、项目落地周期较短的国家，应该优先考虑成立子公司或分公司。周期较长的项目，应充分考虑周期内项目所在国的潜在风险，采取有效的风险防范措施。

2. 大力拓展业务领域

2.1 突出重点，兼顾平衡。进一步巩固石油、天然气、水处理、矿山、基建、新能源六大领域内优势项目的落实，深化水处理、新能源等领域的布局，推进六大领域业务全面开展。

2.2 产品方面，坚持原材料制造、钢管、钢结构业务的基础地位，推进产品向高端、智能及模块化发展。

1.4 We should improve the assessment of country-specific political risks, fully consider the prevention of compliance risks and make prompt adjustments in our businesses. We will give priority to countries with stable political situations, low risks and shorter project implementation cycles when planning to set up new subsidiaries or branch offices. As for any project with a longer cycle, full consideration should be given to potential risks in the country where the project is located during the cycle period, and effective measures should be taken to prevent those risks.

2. Devoting major efforts to expand business sectors

2.1 Emphasis will be placed on key businesses while a healthy balance between all businesses will also be taken into account. We will continue to advance the implementation of competitive projects in such sectors as oil, natural gas, water treatment, mines, infrastructure construction and new energy. We will strengthen our presence in water treatment and new energy, thus advancing the all-round development of our business in the above six sectors.

2.2 As regards our products, we will maintain the fundamental status of raw material manufacturing, steel tubes and steel structures and push ahead with the improvement of our projects, moving towards high-end, smart and modular manufacturing.

2.3 紧跟各国政策导向，基于各国资源禀赋与特点，聚焦核心领域，发展新兴领域，加快前瞻性行业布局步伐。在明确发展方向和路径后组建专业化团队，将局部市场成功经验推广复制，并最终实现核心板块业务模式全球化。

2.4 积极关注新技术发展，充分利用人工智能、区块链、云计算、物联网、大数据、5G 等前沿技术或科学成果，促进公司发展与创新。

3. 不断延伸产业链

3.1 以项目采购服务为基础，强化项目设计、施工、融资、管理的能力。完善现有领域 EPC 项目专业总包、分包、转包的资源配置。做到"拿得到，做得好"。在现有 EPC 业务基础上，向 EPC+ 方向发展升级。

3.2 发展材料研究及应用、工程设计、材料制造、工程管理控制及运营、大

2.3 Keeping up with policy directions of different countries, we will accelerate the forward-looking industrial structuring by focusing on core areas and seeking development in emerging areas according to the resource endowment of different countries. We will build specialized teams once we have identified our development orientation and path, extend the successful practices in regional markets and achieve globalization of the business models of core segments in the end.

2.4 We will pay active attention to the progress of new technologies and make the most of frontier technologies, including but not limited to, artificial intelligence (AI), blockchain, cloud computing, IoT(Internet of Things), big data and 5G, thus advancing the development and innovation of the company.

3. Continuing to extend the industrial chains

3.1 Based on project purchasing services, we will enhance our capabilities of project designing, construction, financing and management. We will optimize the resource allocation in the general contracting and subcontracting of EPC projects in existing areas, ensuring that we are able to "get it and do it well." With our current EPC businesses, we are ready to evolve towards "EPC+"in the future.

3.2 We will advance materials research and application, engineering

宗贸易、全球供应链管理、物流运输、教培研版块等，逐渐形成产学研一体化的全产业链集团化公司。紧密结合市场需求与行业发展趋势，打造设计中心、研发中心、工程项目运营控制中心、全球供应链管理中心、材料制造中心、物流中心等版块，创建全方位、多领域协同发展的格局。

4. 打造专业化的人才队伍

公司竞争力的核心，归根结底是人才的竞争。未来十年，公司将致力于打造一支成梯队、成规模、成体系、成团队的高素质专业化人才队伍。

4.1 加大从国内外知名高校招聘优质毕业生的力度，按照个人专业背景及发展意愿订制完整的培训、培养计划，分领域建立专业技术人才储备中心。为不同部门、不同职能、不同板块储备完整的后备人才。同时，加强综合能力培养，打造专业特长突出，综合能力出众的复合型人才队伍。

design, material manufacturing, engineering management and operation control, trade in bulk commodities, global supply chain management and logistics management as well as education, training and research, gradually forming a whole-industry-chain group company with the integration of industry and research. Paying close attention to market needs and the trends of industrial development, we will set up design center, Research and Development (R&D) center, engineering project operation control center, global supply chain management center, material manufacturing center and logistics center, achieving all-dimensional, multiple-area coordinated development.

4. Building teams of professional talents

A company's competitiveness, in essence, is underpinned by the competitiveness of its talents. In the next ten years, we will devote ourselves to building a considerably large team which, systematically composed of the finest talents, forms an echelon of professionals and displays the power of good teamwork.

4.1 We will redouble our efforts to recruit high-quality graduates from renowned universities both in China and abroad. Detailed plans of training are to be made according to their educational backgrounds and career development orientations. Talent reserve centers for professionals and technical personnel will be established on an area-by-area

4.2 充分发挥合伙人制度的优势，分领域、分板块整合并吸引国内外设计、采购、施工、安装等领域的顶尖人才或专家以个人或团队形式加入。

4.3 坚持以培养人为优先的公司人才储备战略，分阶段培养具有全球视野的综合型项目经理，具有CEO格局的公司核心管理层，实现人才引进与培养相结合的格局。

4.4 完善人才考评体系，坚持优中选优、能者先升的人才晋升通道。对不符合要求的人才，及时调整或调离工作岗位。完善从助理、经理、高级经理到合伙人晋升体系的考评内容。营造"上升无限制，发展无瓶颈"的公司人才晋升体系。

4.5 坚持"利益共享、员工优先"

basis, thus preparing full-range talents for different departments, functions and business segments. In the meanwhile, we will intensify the training of their comprehensive skills and build a team of multiple-skill talents with outstanding professional advantages and comprehensive capabilities.

4.2 We will give full play to the advantages of the partnership system and attract first-class talents or experts in designing, purchasing, construction, installation, etc. both in China and from abroad to join us as individuals or teams.

4.3 We will stick to the strategy of talent reserve prioritizing the training of people, develop multiple-skill project managers with global vision in phases and foster core management with the capability and broad-mindedness of the CEO, thus achieving the combination of talent introduction and training.

4.4 We will improve our talent assessment and evaluation system, while keeping to the promotion channel based on the principle of "picking the best of the best and giving priority to the able ones." Those who fail to meet the requirements of a certain post will be timely transferred to another one. We will refine the assessment methodology for assistants, managers, senior managers and partners, thus establishing a promotion system with "no limitations to upward mobility and no bottleneck in career development."

4.5 We will adhere to the fundamental

的基本分配原则。员工薪酬和分配比例与业绩挂钩，传统业务维持原有分配模式，新业务分配模式依据业务特点调整。能者多劳，劳者多得。进一步完善市场开发激励政策，鼓舞员工奋勇争先开拓市场。

4.6 坚持员工自我教育提升与互相学习进步相结合，人人争当教育家，创建良好的个人成长环境与企业学习氛围。

基于上述理念，公司志在打造一支众志成城、敢于担当、充满活力、激情四射、专业严谨的国际化一流队伍。

5. 布局金融产业，深化资本市场参与度

5.1 以公司的发展战略为引领，借用各类平台、寻找多种融资手段、创新融资工具、丰富融资模式以支持公司业务发展。同时，强化公司资金管理水平，降低公司资金成本。此外，运用金融手段建立并完善风险防控体系。

principle of "shared interests, employees first" in our compensation policies. The compensations people receive are linked with their business performance. The traditional model of compensation will be maintained in existing businesses while adjustments will be made in new businesses according to their characteristics. "The abler one is, the more one should do; the more one does, the more one will receive." We will further improve the incentive policies for market development and encourage people to bravely compete to outperform others.

4.6 Combining self-education and peer learning, every member of CNOOD strives to be an educator, thus creating a good environment for personal growth and a healthy atmosphere of learning for the company as a whole.

Inspired by the above spirit, CNOOD is determined to build a first-class international team, whose vibrant, enthusiastic, professional and rigorous members are united as one and are brave enough to take on responsibilities.

5. Building a network in the financial sector with deeper involvement in the capital market

5.1 Guided by our development strategy, we will support the growth of our businesses by employing various platforms, seeking multiple means of financing, exploring new financing tools and enriching our financing models.

5.2 择机开展投资收购等资本运作，借助专业化运营，建立上市公司孵化制度。以施璐德亚洲有限公司为孵化中心，让成熟的或高度专业化的业务板块适时剥离，形成独立的上市主体。在未来十年要争取建立 8～10 个上市团队，打造 2～3 家上市公司，并建立起各板块上市规划路线图。

5.3 完成金融产业基础布局，汇集优秀的专业人才队伍，初步打造包含银行、保险、信托、基金、融资租赁、财务公司等多种形式的金融产业板块雏形，最终在为公司创收的基础上，实现公司产业结构升级，为公司的永续发展注入不竭动力。

In the meanwhile, we will improve fund management and lower the capital costs. In addition, we will use financial measures to establish and improve our risk prevention and control system.

5.2 We will initiate capital operation including investment and mergers and acquisitions (M&A) at appropriate times and establish incubation mechanism for would-be listed companies by professional operation. With CNOOD as the incubation hub, mature or highly specialized business segments will be stripped in appropriate phases to form independent entities as candidates for listed companies. We will try our best to form eight to ten teams for this task in the next ten years and create two or three listed companies. A road map to the creation of listed companies in respective business segments will also be worked out.

5.3 We will complete the basic network in the financial sector, pool the best professional talents and create a basic financial segment with multiple business forms including banking, insurance, trust, funds, financial leasing and finance companies. While increasing revenue for the company, this also helps to realize industrial upgrading and provide inexhaustible driving force for the sustainable growth of the company.

6. 创新公司治理机制，共治共建未来

6.1 完善董事会建设，坚持董事会领导下的公司治理机制。关系公司发展方向、股东核心利益的问题，坚持股东大会及董事会多数表决相结合的原则。建立完善董事会、股东、员工三者之间的沟通渠道，减少管理成本，提高管理效率。同时，进一步拓宽员工、股东、董事三者间角色转换渠道，对表现杰出的员工给予股权激励，或优先推选为董事。业绩突出的股东，享有股权优先购买权。

6.2 以上市公司的标准，建立健全董事会及高层管理人员的职责及评估制度；进一步优化董事结构，明确董事会的职责与权限，发挥董事会的决策作用，提高公司的决策能力；在董事会内部进行专业分工，使得董事会工作实现专门化；建立董事评估制度，围绕创造长期股东价值，设计涵盖财务、公司战略、人力资源、公共关系等方面的业绩指标；完善独

6. Exploring new mechanisms of corporate governance for a shared future by cooperation and participation

6.1 We will further strengthen the Board of Directors while adhering to the corporate governance mechanism under the leadership of the Board. We uphold the principle of combining the majority decision at the general meeting of shareholders and that at the Board of Directors as regards issues concerning the company's development orientation or the core interests of shareholders. We will establish and improve the communication channel among the Board, shareholders and employees to reduce management costs and enhance efficiency. In the meanwhile, we will further expand the role-switching channels among employees, shareholders and Board members. Employees with outstanding performance will be granted stock options or be given priority in the nomination of candidates for Board members. Shareholders with outstanding performance shall enjoy preemptive rights.

6.2 We will establish and steadily improve the systems of duties and evaluations for the Board of Directors and senior management based on the requirements for a listed company. We will further optimize the composition of Board of Directors, clarify the responsibilities and limits of authority of the Board, give full play to the decision-

立董事制度，增强公司决策的科学性和公正性，最大程度保障股东的利益。

making role of the Board and enhance its decision-making capabilities. Division of work will be carried out within the Board to achieve specialization in its operation. We will establish the assessment and evaluation system for Board members, which, focusing on long-term shareholder value, includes performance indicators of financial status, corporate strategy, human resources and public relations. We will improve the system of independent directors to help the company to make decisions in a scientific and impartial manner, thus fully protecting the interests of our shareholders.

6.3 未来十年，公司将积极推进区块链管理，继续深化扁平化管理等理念与架构的实施，以标准化与集成化相结合的方式，以操作手册和Workbench为主要方式，创新公司治理机制，力求实现高效决策、专业发展，形成别具特色的共同决策、共同治理、共同发展的有机生态系统。

6.3 In the next ten years, CNOOD will actively promote blockchain management and continue to further the implementation of managerial concepts and architectures such as flat management. Combining standardization and integration, we will use work manuals and Workbench as the primary means to explore new mechanisms of corporate governance and achieve highly efficient decision-making and specialized development, thus forming a unique organic ecosystem whose members act in concert to make decisions, perform management tasks and achieve development.

- 操作手册

基于扁平化的组织架构，公司以标准化的操作流程为运行机制，实现了管理与效率的高度统一；建立一系列完善的操作手册，用于规范和指导相关工作，防控公司风险。未来将紧密结合公司发展规划，及时对操作手册进行补充、迭代和升级。

- Work-manuals

Based on a flat organization architecture, CNOOD, with the standardized operation process as its functioning mechanism, has achieved a high degree of combination of management and efficiency. We have formulated and refined a series of work

- Workbench

公司自主开发的 Workbench，将进一步广纳意见，持续提升，以实现平台做大做强、全球行业内知名的阶段性目标。在十年中后期，平台将有计划逐步对外开放。公司将通过政策性引导，持续加强 Workbench 在公司运行及管理中的作用，提高公司运行效率。

未来十年，Workbench 将致力于实现以下功能：

（1）保持快速迭代。根据公司战略规划、业务发展、公司管理的需求，快速响应并升级完善系统。

（2）加强多终端研发。适配各类终端设备，提升使用便捷性和交互体验。

（3）实现"智慧CNOOD"。通过互联网、大数据和人工智能能技术，推进公司业务系统化、管理科学化、架构扁平

manuals to provide norms and guidance for relevant businesses and control company-level risks. In the future, work manuals will be promptly supplemented, iterated and upgraded in line with the development plans of the company.

- Workbench

We will further pool wisdom to constantly enhance Workbench, which is independently developed by CNOOD, to achieve its phased goal of growing bigger and stronger and becoming globally renowned in the industry. At a later stage within the next ten years, the platform will gradually become open to outside users. We will continuously reinforce, through the guidance of company-level policies, the role of Workbench in the daily operation and management of the company, thus improving overall operating efficiency.

In the next ten years, Workbench attempts to realize the following functions:

A. Keeping up rapid iteration. It will rapidly respond to the needs of the company's strategic planning, business development and corporate management by upgrading and improving the system.

B. Intensify R&D in multiple-terminal application. It is to be adapted to various types of terminal devices to enhance user-friendliness and improve the interaction experience.

C. Realizing "Intelligent CNOOD." It aims to promote business systematization, scientific management and flat

化，为公司发展和决策以及管理层产生提供支持。

（4）打造行业生态系统。构建大数据一体化平台，接入行业伙伴。提高协作效率和品质，助力行业协同发展。

7. 加强党建工作，凝聚发展动力

7.1 突出主题，创新载体，加强党的思想建设。积极发挥党员先锋模范作用，团结并带领公司不畏艰难，开拓进取，铸造辉煌。

7.2 加强领导，完善机制，加强党的组织建设。积极探索"支部建在项目上"的组织形式，充分发挥党支部的战斗堡垒作用，加强公司的集体凝聚力，用支部建设推动公司生产力发展。

organization architecture by drawing on technologies such as Internet, big data and artificial intelligence (AI), providing support for the development and decision-making of the company as well as the appointment of managerial personnel.

D. Building an industry-level ecosystem. It aims to create an integrated platform of big data, which is accessible to industrial partners. It is supposed to enhance the efficiency and quality of cooperation and boost the coordinated development of the industry.

7. Improving Party (CPC) building as a driver of growth

7.1 We will highlight the theme and explore new ways of strengthening the ideological work of the Party. Giving full play to the exemplary and vanguard role of Party members, we will unite and lead all CNOODers in the fearless, pioneering efforts for a bright future.

7.2 We will improve our leadership and refine the mechanism to consolidate the organizations of the Party. We will actively explore the forms of "building Party branches on the projects," bring into full play the role of Party branch committees as "militant bastions," promote the collective cohesion of the company and enhance company-level productivity by the building of Party branch committees.

8. 重视企业社会责任，创造和谐美好家园

8.1 探索建立终身教育体制、退休养老福利体系等关系员工终身幸福的教育、福利制度，为子孙后代建立完善的成长、成才通道，为全体员工提供安心舒适的生活环境。

8.2 积极参与希望工程等各类社会福利及慈善事业，为全人类的共同发展做出贡献。

五、结语

未来十年，将是公司发展至关重要的阶段，我们将齐心协力，强化公司创造价值的能力，推动公司发展进入快车道。

秉承相互关心、创造开心的企业文化，帮助人、培养人、成就人，为把公司建设成为幼有所育、学有所教、劳有所得、病有所医、老有所养、住有所居、弱有所扶的施璐德人利益共同体、事业共同体、命运共同体而不断奋斗。

8. Paying great attention to corporate social responsibility (CSR) and creating a harmonious, beautiful home for us all

8.1 We will explore the possibility of establishing education and welfare systems concerning the lifelong happiness of all CNOODers, including the systems of lifelong education and retirement welfare. We aim to establish channels of growth for our children and grandchildren and provide comfortable living conditions for all CNOODers.

8.2 We will actively participate in various social welfare and charity causes such as "Project Hope," making contributions to human progress.

V. Concluding Remarks

The next ten years will be a period of crucial importance for the development of the company. We will work in full cooperation and with unity of purpose, strengthen the value-creating capabilities of the company and push it into a fast track of growth.

Embracing the corporate culture of "caring for each other and creating a new ocean of delightfulness," we work hard to help, train and fulfill people and strive tirelessly to build the company into a community of shared interests, shared cause and shared future where all CNOODers have access to childcare, education, employment, medical services, elderly care, housing and social assistance.

写在施璐德十周年
On the 10th Anniversary of the Founding of CNOOD

■ Dennis Chi

"酒酣胸胆尚开张，鬓微霜，又何妨！持节云中，何日遣冯唐？会挽雕弓如满月，西北望，射天狼。"

2019年，施璐德十周年。然而，这里的黎明静悄悄，没有仪式，没有庆祝，有的是沉思和反思；有的是教训，深刻的教训。自私、自大、自狂、自傲，对公司的发展极其有害；无私、冷静、谦虚、决断，是公司生存的基石。这十年，是进步和发展的十年，洗礼了公司共创、共治、共享文化，历练了一批勇于进取的志士，锻炼了几支能够管控实施复杂项目的团队，为施璐德未来的发展，创造了无限的可能性。

Heart gladdened with strong wine, who cares
For a few frosted hairs?
When will the imperial court send
Me as envoy with flags and banners? Then I'll bend
My bow like a full moon, and aiming northwest, I
Will shoot down the Wolf from the sky.

The year 2019 witnesses the 10th anniversary of the founding of CNOOD. "The dawns here are quiet," however, with no ceremonies or celebrations. We have nothing but contemplation, reflection and lessons — profound lessons. Selfishness, conceit, arrogance or haughtiness is extremely detrimental to the company's growth; selflessness, calmness, modesty and decisiveness are the cornerstones of its survival. The past ten years have been a period of progress and development, during which we have refined the corporate

有的人问施璐德为什么存在。

我们为爱而生，因爱而存。为了一群守信用、有爱心、想奋斗，致力于实现自身价值的人，创造的一个实现梦想的地方，创造的一个人人爱之、惜之、趋之的梦想之地。公司初创，条件有限，新人成长，不太成熟，合伙背景，千差万别，合伙文化，不一而足。公司虽致力于成就人、培养人，但对不同人的帮助有限，更多需要的是自适应、自成长、自生长。对于实在不能磨合、不能融入、不能适应的同仁，公司欢迎尽快另谋出路，公司竭尽所能，能帮则帮，能扶则扶。

我们同事之间的关系呢？

进入施璐德的同事，我们的关系是家人，是合伙人，或者即将成长为成熟的合伙人。在公司里，我们有职责的区分，业务、财务、融资、商务、法务、风险、人

culture of a company created, managed and shared by all its members, tempered a number of people of integrity and ideals who are brave enough to break new ground and trained teams which are able to manage and carry out complex projects, thus creating infinite possibilities for CNOOD to grow in the future.

Some people would ask why CNOOD exists.

We were born for the sake of love and exist for the sake of love too. CNOOD is a place created for a group of affectionate people who keep their word, want to make endeavors and work hard to realize their value; it is a dreamland which everyone loves, cherishes and gravitates to. During its initial stage of growth, we were not in a favorable situation. New members were still immature, while the backgrounds and cultures varied greatly among the partners. Though we have been working hard to produce and train talents, the help we could provide for different people is insufficient. Instead they would have to depend more on self-adaptation, self-development and self-growth. For those who are really unable to fit in, we encourage them to look for new jobs as soon as possible while we do our best to help and support them.

What about the relations between our colleagues?

All the colleagues in CNOOD are members of one family; we are all partners or would-be partners. Within the company, we are divided by different

事、技术、质量等等；在团队里，我们有角色的不同，根据项目的不同，角色会有所差别。但实质上，我们都是合伙人，为了共同的事业走到一起，为了互相成全、互相成就，我们走到一起。我们互相包容。团队是无限的，合伙人根据自己的业务特点、每个人的特点，组织自己的团队。合适，则聚；不合适，则分。在团队里，业务合伙人有完全的人事权和财权；在项目上面，项目经理有完全的人事权和财权。每个人都可以组织自己的团队，建立自己的独特业务体系。在公司里，在团队内，在项目上，互相尊重为合作前提，没有尊重，就没有合作。

特别说说不同部门之间的关系。我们很多合伙人来自不同的公司，有国企、外企、民企、私企等等，文化背景差别非常。来到施璐德以后，请大家尽量忘掉以前文化中不好的地方，尽量发挥积极的地方，这就会最终形成施璐德文化的一部分。请大家尽量想他人所想，急他人所急，尽量站在公司发展层面，来看待问题，解决问题。我想，如果这样，公司的冲突会少很多；解决问题，会有完全不同的好思路、好方法。

positions and responsibilities—business, financial affairs, funding, commercial affairs, legal affairs, risk management, human resources, technology, quality control, etc. In teams, we assume different roles according to different projects. However, essentially we are all partners who have joined together for a common cause and help each other to achieve our goals and fulfill ourselves. We forgive each other. Teams are boundless; partners organize their own teams according to their unique businesses and individual characters. We get together if we fit each other; we get divided if not. Within any team, the business partner has full authority over human and financial resources; on any project, the project manager has full authority over human and financial resources. Everyone can organize a team and establish a unique business system. No matter within the company, in a team or on a project, mutual respect is a prerequisite for cooperation; it would be impossible to cooperate without respect.

Now a few words about the relations between departments within the company. Many of our partners came from different companies, including state-owned enterprises (SOEs), foreign-capital companies, private companies, etc., with huge differences in their cultural backgrounds. Having joined CNOOD, please try your best to forget the negative elements of your previous workplace and give full play to the positive ones,

我们第一次推出了自己定义自己的职责,同时,会尝试针对对应的职责,对每个人建立评价体系。为什么?

我们有很好的、很出色的合伙人,但是也很有限,越来越多的同事需要不断进步,满足不同市场发展的需要,满足不同业务发展的需要。我们的项目,我们的同事,分布在不同的国家和区域。公司的不同业务板块,也分布在不同的地方。同事很难聚集,培训很难开展,指令很难下达,规定很难实行。如果做好业务、规范管理、高效运营,是摆在公司所有同事面前的一个很直接问题。公司经营不善,大家都得找工作,因此,这个问题,不是某一个人的问题,而是我们所有同事共同的问题。所谓成长,就是思考问题、直面问题、解决问题。做得越多,做得越好,成长越快。我们自定义职责,就是共创、共治、共享的一个举措。让公司的方方面面,都有人看、有人思、有人管、有人做,不怕重复。大家都在思考中进步,在共管中成长。我们力求尽快实现,Workbench 对我们成长的跟踪,对成长好的、成长快的、品德好的、愿意为公司奉

which will eventually become a part of the CNOOD culture. Try your best to understand what others are thinking and share their concerns; try your best to look at various problems from the perspective of the company's development. If we do so, I believe, we will have much fewer conflicts within the company, and we will have totally different, excellent ways of solving problems.

We are the first company to have proposed the idea of "self-defined responsibilities" and in the meantime attempt to set up an assessment system for every member according to their individual responsibilities. Why?

While we have great partners, we do not have enough of them. More and more colleagues need to make continuous progress to meet the growing needs in different markets and businesses. Our projects and colleagues are distributed across different countries and regions. Our business segments, too, are distributed in different places. It is hard to assemble our colleagues, to carry out training programs, to give orders or to implement rules and regulations. By what means are we going to achieve good results in our businesses with standardized management and efficient operation? This is a question of immediate importance encountered by all our colleagues. We will have to look for new jobs if the company fails to deliver good performance. Therefore, this is not a problem for one person but a problem all our colleagues have to face.

献的人，给予更多锻炼和成长的机会，逐步晋升到领导岗位、关键岗位、核心岗位。既给个人成长机会，给个人创造未来，更给公司创造可以信赖的未来，给我们大家创造更加可靠的未来。

很多人问为什么看起来和CEO李燕飞女士没有关系的业务，也需要给她发提成。

她不仅是我很好的业务伙伴，同时，她还是我推举出来的CEO，实际只有1美元的年薪。她过去几年的管理工作，大家有目共睹。她节约了大家的时间，更节约了我的时间。有个玩笑话，所有难做的项目，难做的事情，所有的人都可以跑，而我跑不了。从而我有更多的时间来从事业务的开发，从事项目的跟踪，从事合同的签署。这也是公司生存的理由之一，很

Growth means thinking about problems, facing them bravely and solving them. The more and the better we do, the faster we will grow. The idea of "self-defined responsibilities" is one of the measures for building a company created, managed and shared by all its members. We must ensure that every aspect of the company be taken care of, and we are not afraid of repetition. All of us are making progress as thinkers; we grow while sharing responsibilities of management. We try our best to enable, as soon as possible, Workbench to track our growth, giving more opportunities to those who grow better and faster, maintain higher moral standards and are willing to contribute to the development of the company, and promoting them to key leadership positions. By doing so, we are able to create a future for every member by providing them with opportunities of growth, while also creating a more reliable future for the company and for us all.

Many people ask why our CEO Fay Lee gets a percentage for businesses that seem to have nothing to do with her.

She is a very good business partner for me, as well as the CEO of CNOOD recommended by me. In fact, she receives an annual salary of one dollar. The great management job she has done during the past years is obvious to all. She has saved everyone's time, in particular mine. I once joked that everyone could avoid a difficult project or a knotty problem

重要的理由。希望大家的时间拿来做好项目，跟踪好客户。有一点大家可以放心，公司给大家的，就是公司能够给的最好的，公司一直就是以个人利益为优先。CEO 李燕飞女士，同样是靠业务提成来取得收入。她的业务能力很强，如果不做 CEO，她的业务会很好，收入会高很多，会超过她现在的若干倍。至少比我强很多，譬如某个客户，我跟踪了 5 年都没有做出来，但她开始跟踪后，半年时间就出了很好的效果。窥一斑而见全豹，由此我们可以窥见她的业务能力。我要感谢她为我们大家的付出，大家也应该感谢她为我们大家做的努力。

说说个人的发展。在考虑这个问题的时候，请大家务必记住，施璐德是一个合伙制的公司，公司将成为每个人的一部分。

公司的合伙人越来越多。合伙人如何发展？一般而言，合伙人都有很好的技术背景、专业背景等，都有很好的资源优势，有的资源优势甚至是合伙人自己都完全没有意识到。从狭义方面来讲，每个合

except me. Thanks to her work, I have more time to develop business, follow projects and sign contracts. This is also one—probably the most important one—of the reasons that CNOOD still exists. You are expected to spend your time on doing projects and following your clients. You can rest assured that the company always gives you the best it is able to offer; we always put individual interests first. Fay Lee, as the CEO, earns her income by commissions just like other colleagues. With her exceptional business abilities, she would provide superior performance in business, and her income would be several times what she earns now if she were not the CEO. At least she is much better than me. For example, I myself followed one client for five years without success, and she delivered remarkable results only half a year after she took over. As the saying goes, from a single instance you may infer the whole. We can see her ability from this case. I would express my gratitude to her for what she has done for us; I think all of us should thank her for the efforts she has made for us.

A few words about individual career development. When thinking about this issue, bear in mind that CNOOD is a partnership which will become a part of everyone.

We are having more and more partners. How are they supposed to achieve their career development? Generally speaking, partners all have good technical and professional backgrounds

伙人事实上都可以和我共建一个公司，而且这个公司可以运营得很好。为什么呢？我除了不懂业务，其他公司运营方面都经过专业训练和锻炼，能力属于中上，综合水平可以推动公司的良性发展。这就是施璐德的优势：不同的合伙人之间，各自发挥不同的优势，充分分享各自的优势，就会形成各具特色的业务板块；业务板块的发展，会有更多的溢出效应，衍生出更多的业务板块。合伙人可以根据自身的特点和喜好，推动和带动或者主导某一种或者某几种业务板块的发展，形成自身独特的价值实现模式。性灵出万象，风骨超常伦。只要我们放下身段，实事求是、彼此尊重、真心合作、百花齐放、百家争鸣，指日可待。

公司的非合伙人如何发展呢？如果有成熟方向的，可以参照合伙人模式。如果没有成熟方向的，可以加入任一合伙人的团队，和合伙人一起发展，协助合伙人开展业务，并不断学习成长。在此过程中，努力发现自己的兴趣方向，并使之不

as well as advantages in resources, some of which have not yet been recognized even by the partners themselves. From a narrow perspective, every partner in fact is able to co-establish a company with me and run it very well. Why? I am well trained and tested in operating a company except for technical expertise, and my above-average ability enables me to realize the sustainable development of the company. This is the advantage of CNOOD: different partners can harness and share their respective advantages, thus creating numerous business segments with distinctive characteristics; the development of business segments will produce stronger spill-over effect and in turn bring about more business segments. Partners could push and lead the growth of one or more business segments according to what they are good at and what they like, forming specific models of value creation. "It is your temperament that shapes your demeanor and your character that transcends the ordinary." As long as we lower ourselves and be realistic, respect each other and work together sincerely, it can be expected that "a hundred flowers blooming and a hundred schools of thought contending" will soon be a reality.

As for the non-partner members, how will they achieve career development? For anyone with a mature orientation, the partnership model could be followed. Anyone without a mature orientation can join the team of a partner, develop with

断成熟。一旦成熟，就可以参照合伙人发展模式。兴趣是关键，一个人成就最高的地方，应该是他最感兴趣的地方，应该是他舍得投入全部精力、为它不懈奋斗的地方。每个人的成熟，有他自己的轨迹，给自己时间，不盲从、不妄动、多思考、勤努力、常学习，必有云开日出的时候。长风破浪会有时，直挂云帆济沧海。

财务、商务、总务、质量、体系、系统等等，这些同事如何发展呢？归根结底，根据自己的兴趣方向，不断学习新知识，结合公司的发展方向，不断提升自身的能力和水平，为公司的发展提供新的发展动力和支撑，为发展保驾护航，成为某一行业的领军者，成为某一学科的领头羊，成为某一新行业的规划者、倡导者、实践者、成就者。

未来，我们将继续以培养人为核心，以培养特色团队为导向，以培养有担当、

the partner and assist in carrying out businesses, while keeping learning and growing. They are expected to try their best to discover the fields in which they are really interested and become more and more mature. Once mature enough, the partnership model could be followed. Interest is of crucial importance. People make the greatest achievement in areas where they are most interested and willing to put in all their energy and work relentlessly. People have their own paths towardss maturity. Take your time, and never follow others blindly and impetuously; think more, work hard, and learn on a constant basis, and you will finally see the sunshine, just as Li Bai, the famous Tang-dynasty poet once wrote, "A time will come to ride the wind and cleave the waves; I'll set my cloud-like sail and cross the sea which raves."

What about the career development of our colleagues dealing with financial affairs, commercial affairs, general affairs, quality control, systems, etc.? To put it in a nutshell, they should keep learning new knowledge according to their interests and improve their capabilities in light of the orientation of the company, giving new motive power and support to the company's development. They are encouraged to become leaders in their sectors and professions and the planners, sponsors, practitioners and achievers in new industries.

In the future, we will continue to focus on training people, be oriented

敢担当、奋勇争先的领导力量为目标，造就人才，造就施璐德的持续发展的未来，为把施璐德建设成为人人爱之、惜之、趋之的梦想之地而持续努力。

towardss the fostering of teams with distinguished features and aim to create leadership with the courage of taking on responsibilities and competing for the best. Determined to produce talents and provide CNOOD with a future of sustainable development, we will continue to strive for building CNOOD into a dreamland which everyone loves, cherishes and gravitates to.

池勇海
Dennis Chi

池勇海，男，汉族，1970年生于湖北省仙桃市。武汉理工大学管理学硕士，硕士导师刘国新教授；复旦大学经济学博士，博士生导师洪远朋教授。2008年创立施璐德亚洲有限公司，现担任施璐德亚洲有限公司董事长。

Dennis Chi, male, ethnic Han, was born in Xiantao, Hubei Province in 1970. He received his master's degree in management from Wuhan University of Technology, where he studied under Professor Liu Guoxin, and received his Ph.D. in Economics from Fudan University, where he studied under Professor Hong Yuanpeng. Dennis is now Chairman of CNOOD Asia Limited, which he founded in 2008.

《共同利益论——基于国际经济视角》
新书发布会成功举办

Common Interest Theory — Based on International Economic Perspective
Launched in Success

■ 2019 年 10 月 27 日

2019 年 10 月 27 日下午，施璐德亚洲有限公司董事长池勇海博士的《共同利益论——基于国际经济视角》新书发布会在骏莱海鲜鱼港三楼宴会厅成功举办。发布会由复旦大学经济学院、复旦大学出版社主办，复旦大学泛海书院、施璐德亚洲有限公司承办，复旦大学经济学院博士生导师、复旦大学泛海书院常务副院长严法善教授主持。

On the afternoon of October 27, 2019, a press conference was held successfully at the banquet hall of Jun Lai Seafood Hotel for the release of *Common Interest Theory— Based on International Economic Perspective*, a new book by Dr. Dennis Chi, chairman of CNOOD Asia Limited. The event was sponsored by the School of Economics of Fudan University and Fudan University Press and organized by Fanhai Academy of Fudan University and CNOOD. It was chaired by Yan Fashan, a doctoral supervisor at the School of Economics of Fudan University and the executive deputy director of Fanhai Academy.

嘉宾致辞   Guest Speeches

洪远朋
复旦大学经济学院
资深教授

Hong Yuanpeng
Senior professor at the
School of Economics of
Fudan University

张晖明
复旦大学经济学院
经济系主任、教授

Zhang Huiming
Professor and director
of the Economics
Department under the
School of Economics
of Fudan University

徐惠平
复旦大学出版社副总编辑

Xu Huiping
Deputy editor-in-chief
of Fudan University
Press

陶友之
上海社会科学院
研究员

Tao Youzhi
Researcher at
Shanghai Academy of
Social Sciences

马 艳
上海财经大学政治经济学系主任、教授

Ma Yan
Professor and director of the Political Economy
Department of Shanghai University of Finance and
Economics

陈 波
上海财经大学经济学院教授
Chen Bo
Professor at the School of Economics of
Shanghai University of Finance and Economics

陈飞翔
上海交通大学安泰经济与管理学院教授
Chen Feixiang
Professor at Antai College of Economics &
Management of Shanghai Jiao Tong University

文 玲
海南波罗密信息科技有限公司
董事长
Wen Ling
Chairwoman of Hainan Parami
Information Technology Co. Ltd

陈诗一
复旦大学经济学院党委书记、教授
Chen Shiyi
Party secretary of the School of
Economics of Fudan University

复旦校友代表
Fudan alumni representative

作者发言

池勇海先生的部分发言：

施璐德十年的实践，施璐德学会第一本书——《共同利益论——基于国际经济视角》，在尊敬的导师洪远朋教授的指导和关心下，在复旦大学出版社的努力支持下，顺利面世。感谢复旦，感恩恩师。

感谢陈波教授，感谢杨文宇师兄，感谢叶正茂师兄，以及所有指导、关心、帮助我的师兄师姐。

Author's Speech

Excerpts of Dr. Dennis Chi's speech:

Under the guidance and care of my well-beloved mentor Professor Hong Yuanpeng and with the great support from Fudan University Press, *Common Interest Theory —Based on International Economic Perspective*, the first book of the CNOOD Society that sums up the practice of CNOOD over the past 10 years, has been published pretty smoothly. I am really grateful to Fudan University and my mentor Professor Hong.

I would also like to thank Professor Chen Bo, senior schoolmates Yang Wenyu and Ye Zhengmao and all fellow schoolmates who have given me guidance, care and help.

从洪老师给我指定这个题目起，到今年是十周年。我们做了两件事：一是成立了施璐德公司；二是在全球实践这个理论。今天很荣幸能够作为一个十年总结发布此书。

《共同利益论》涵盖理论发展、国际贸易、跨国投资、人力资源的跨国流动，以及对我国"一带一路"倡议的实践意义。由于我的水平极其有限，没有对十年来的实践做高度洗练的总结，仅做了初步的探索。十年的实践内容，将会更加丰富，更加生动，同时更加复杂。

It has been 10 years since Professor Hong assigned me this research topic. In this period, we have accomplished two things: setting up the CNOOD and practicing the theory all over the world. I'm honored to have this book published today as a summary of our performance over the 10 years.

Common Interest Theory covers such topics as theoretical development, international trade, transnational investment and transnational flows of human resources as well as the theory's practical significance to China's Belt and Road Initiative. Due to my limited knowledge and ability, I have not yet made a highly concise summary of the past 10 years and instead have only carried out preliminary explorations. The 10 years of practice are richer, more vivid and more complex in reality.

池勇海先生与恩师洪远朋教授、师母周老师合影

Mr. Dennis Chi taking a group photo with his tutor Professor Hong Yuanpeng and Ms. Zhou, wife of Professor Hong Yuanpeng

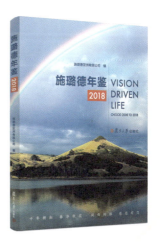

没有办不好的事 上下齐心事便成
We'll Make It with One Mind

■ Heron Tang

不经不觉我加入了施璐德大家庭已第三个年头了。从毕业后一直在银行里工作,三年前我毅然放弃在银行工作,走进私人企业里工作,推动我做出决定的,主要是以下两个原因;其一,是被Dennis的诚意感动了,感谢Dennis三次邀请我加入施璐德这个温暖的大家庭;其二,在我还是施璐德的银行客户经理时,每次到

It has been three years since I joined the big family of CNOOD. After graduation, I had been working in a bank. I gave up my bank job to embrace this private company for two reasons. First, I was deeply struck by Dennis, a man of great sincerity. I am grateful to Dennis, who invited me three times to join this

上海拜访他们，都感觉施璐德这家企业与众不同，特别是从其同事与同事的眼神中，感觉到这间企业的同事之间没有一点儿隔膜，他们的相处像一家人似的，众志成城、充满热诚及干劲去经营这家企业。施璐德给我的感觉是一家朝气勃勃、同事之间相处非常融洽的企业。

没有办不好的事情，上下齐心事便成，施璐德各人凭着这信念，不断接受新挑战，勇往直前地走下去。

warm family of CNOOD. Second, when I worked as a bank customer manager, I had business contact with CNOOD. Every time I visited it in Shanghai, I could feel CNOOD was quite different from others. I saw in the eyes of its staff workers that they were never alienated but got along like a family. They managed the business with great enthusiasm. In my eyes, CNOOD was a youthful business where everyone got along well with each other.

Nothing is impossible if we are of one mind. Backed with this belief, the CNOOD people are united as one to meet one challenge after another and move forward dauntlessly.

邓佩铙
Heron Tang

苏格兰爱丁堡纳皮尔大学硕士，主修市场营销学。2017年7月加入施璐德集团担任集团司库。从事银行工作超过二十年，曾于香港多家跨国银行工作，在跨国企业银行融资及贸易融资具有丰富的经验。拥有设立贸易融资操作部门经验，曾担任贸易融资部门主管；拥有多年跨国企业银行融资及大宗商品贸易融资经验；拥有设计结构性贸易融资产品经验。

考获专业资格：
国际商会CDCS认证专家资格；香港证券及期货事务监察委员会的证券交易牌照1号及就期货合约提供意见给客户牌照5号。

Heron Tang got her master's degree in marketing from Edinburgh Napier University, Scotland. She joined CNOOD in July 2017 to serve as the treasurer of the company. Heron TANG had been engaged in the banking sector for more than 20 years. She worked in a number of multinational banks in Hong Kong and has extensive knowledge of bank financing and trade finance for multinational enterprises. She has rich experience in establishing and leading the trade finance department. She has had years of experience in bank financing and bulk commodity finance for multinational companies. She is expertised in designing structured trade finance products.

Her professional qualifications:
The International Chamber of Commerce (ICC) Certified Documentary Credit Specialists (CDCS) certification; Type 1 licence for dealing in securities and Type 4 licence for advising on securities from Hong Kong Securities and Futures commission.

施璐德数字化升级实践

Digital Upgrading in CNOOD

■ Ken Xu & Nick Zhang

自2015年"互联网+"首次被提出以来，越来越多的传统企业正在慢慢向数字化升级，在这种大升级的浪潮下很多互联网公司也相继涌入，包括阿里巴巴、腾讯、华为等，同时也产生了很多新的名词，如近两年的"产业互联网"、阿里巴巴提出的"大中台、小前台"。对于传统企业而言升级是一个必然的趋势，而如何升级却是因人而异的，不能一蹴而就，比如很多中小企业本身信息化还没做好就开始要做产业互联、要做大中台。一门心思只做信息化不闻窗外事也是不对的，这样很容易跟不上时代的步伐。因此这里我们想结合近几年在施璐德的实践来聊聊如何升级这个问题。

Since the concept of "Internet Plus" was introduced in 2015, more and more traditional companies have launched digital upgrading. Many internet companies have flocked in this great tide of upgrading, including Alibaba, Tencent and Huawei. There have also emerged many new terms over the years, such as "industrial internet" and "big middle-end and small front-end" put forward by Alibaba. Upgrading is an inevitable trend for traditional enterprises. However, how to upgrade varies from business to business. It can't be done overnight. For example, it's wrong for many small and medium-sized enterprises to engage in cross-industry businesses and expand the middle-end before they have achieved information-based development. It is also incorrect to focus only on information technology while neglecting others because they are likely to lag behind the times in this way. Here,

起初在我们来之前，公司已经在尝试做数字化升级。当时公司买过几款项目管理类的软件，但是没有用起来，主要是因为这几款都是私有部署的 C/S 架构的传统软件。私有部署的一般需要有专业的维护人员而且需要购买服务器等硬件，公司如果没有专业的人员一般不建议采用私有部署。而早期的 C/S 架构的软件，客户端安装复杂，交互不友好且不支持移动端，无法满足项目管理这种需要多人异地协作的场景。既然传统软件不适合，那 SaaS 产品是否可以呢？对于一般企业，SaaS 产品应该是不错的选择，可以简单快速地实现信息化。但是，随着企业的不断扩大，各种各样的软件需求也逐渐增多，如果每种都购买 SaaS 产品那就会不可避免地造成产品之间相互独立、无法共享数据。最后，企业还是不得不选择自研，建立自己的研发团队。

we'd like to have a few words on how to upgrade in the light of the CNOOD practice over the years.

Before we joined, CNOOD had already been trying digital upgrading. It had bought some project management software but did not know how to put them into use because these were traditional software with a privately deployed C/S architecture. Private deployment normally requires professional maintenance personnel, as well as such hardware as servers. It is not recommended for companies without professional staff. Besides, early C/S architecture software involves complicated client-side installations, unfriendly interactions and nonsupport to the mobile side. In brief, it was unable to satisfy project management, a scene that requires multi-person off-site collaboration. Now that the traditional software is unfit, will the

2015 年年初，我们加入了施璐德，准备自研系统，首先开发的就是项目管理系统，经过几次的推倒重来，系统最终上线了，我们将其命名为 Workbench。Workbench 从一开始我们就是以 SaaS 模式和平台模式来设计的，因此初期主要开发通用的功能。对于企业定制化的功能，我们先分析一下是否可以转化为通用功能，如果不能，我们会先记录下来，等到后面这些功能积累得多了，我们会考虑重新开发一款产品来解决这些需求。在架构方面，我们考虑的主要是轻量，采用前后端分离的方式，前端采用组件化的方式，后端采用服务化的方式，基础设施方面采用第三方的云计算产品，如云服务器、对象存储、CDN 等。

Workbench 上线后，同事们在使用过

SaaS product work? For most companies, the SaaS product is a good choice, as it achieves information-based operation in a simple, quick way. However, as enterprises are expanding, they need a variety of software. If they apply the SaaS product for each scenario, the products will be mutually independent, unable to share data. In the end, they still have to develop the software by themselves and set up their own R&D teams.

In early 2015, we joined CNOOD to develop our own systems. The first one we worked out was the project management system. After rounds of scrapping and starting all over again, we finally launched the system, naming it Workbench. From the very beginning, we designed Workbench with the SaaS mode and the platform mode. At the start, we focused on developing general functions. As for customized functions, we first analyzed whether we could convert them into general functions. If not, we would keep records first. When we have accumulated more functions, we would develop a product to address all these needs. In terms of architecture, we considered the light weight and separated the front-end and the rear-end. The rear-end adopted the service-oriented mode, while the front-end applied the module-based pattern. The third-party cloud computing products were adopted for the infrastructure, such as cloud servers, object storage and CDN.

After Workbench was launched, our

程中纷纷提出各种需求，我们将需求梳理一下发现要做的事情来了，如客户管理系统、财务系统、审批系统、个人中心等。但我们没有立即开始做这些系统，我们想后面肯定还会有各种各样不同的系统，我们需要提炼出一些可以复用的部分，这样可以提高后续系统的开发效率，同时需要让系统之间更好地实现对接，从而达到数据及功能的共享。因此，我们接下来开发了认证中心和 API 中心，同时将 Workbench 的登录认证迁移到认证中心，为了安全，将协议改为了 HTTPS，登录也加了二次验证。

接下来就是各种系统的开发，同样地，每个系统我们仍旧以 SaaS 模式和平台模式来设计。为了更快速地开发我们做了一些脚手架，方便我们快速搭建一个系统框架。前端部分为了更好地组件化、工程化，我们开发了自己的构建工具。为了更方便地开发、运维和部署，我们搭建了 CI/CD 平台来达到各个流程的自动化、标准化。其间，为了回馈开源社区同时提高公司影响力，我们一直持续地将一些技术开源，也参与了一些其他的开源项目。

co-workers put forward various demands in the process of application. We sorted them out to see what to develop next, such as the customer management system, the financial system, the approval system and the personal center. However, we didn't set out with these systems right away, as we believed there would be various systems to come. We should extract some reusable parts to improve the efficiency of development later. We should also make the systems better dock for data and function sharing. As a result, we developed the authentication center and the API center and shifted Workbench login authentication to the authentication center. To ensure security, we changed the protocol to HTTPS and added second verification at login.

Then we developed various systems. We continued to design each system with the SaaS mode and the platform mode. To develop them faster, we made some scaffolds so that we could quickly build a framework for the system. In the front-end part, we developed our own build tools for better modularization and engineering. To facilitate the development, operation and maintenance, and deployment, we set up a CI/CD platform for automation and standardization in each process. In this period, to reward the open source community and increase our company's influence, we continuously disclosed sources of some technologies and participated in some other open source projects.

2019年是施璐德成立十周年，我们各自家中也分别迎来了新的小成员，很具里程碑意义。在这一年里，我们仍旧保持快速地迭代开发，同时又发布了多个新的系统，推出了移动版的 Workbench。我还有幸参与了《施璐德十年发展纲领》的调研和制订，为公司未来的发展出谋划策。为了准备 SaaS 产品的对外开放，我们拿长沙和本溪的两家公司作为试水，为其提供了 SaaS 版财务系统和 ERP 系统，同时与同行业的公司进行技术和业务交流，从中发现新的需求和我们目前产品的不足。

最后，我们想聊一聊中台。我们认为中台是一步步发展出来的，不能为了中台做中台。我们现在的系统都是根据业务拆分出来的一个个小的应用，应用之间通过服务调用的方式进行通信，服务调用通过统一的认证中心进行认证授权。像我们目前这种架构，业内一般称为"微服务"，而且这种架构在互联网公司很常见。随着业务平台的不断增多，为了增加复用性，需要将一些核心业务以共享服务中心的形式向下沉淀，从而形成一套综合的能力平台即中台。因此，中台一定是企业的业务平台规模达到一定的量，企业的组织方式也一定是平台型的，便于业务平台向下沉淀，最终形成一个前台不断适应变化、中台不断稳固的良性循环。

The year 2019 marks the 10th anniversary of the founding of CNOOD. We've also welcomed new members in our respective families. So it is a milestone for us all. We'll maintain the rapid iterative development. We have released several new systems and launched the mobile Workbench. We are honored to participate in the research and formulation of the Ten-year Development Program of CNOOD, giving counsel on its future development. To prepare for releasing the SaaS product, we have experimented with two companies in Changsha and Benxi, providing them with the SaaS version of the financial system and ERP system. Meanwhile, we have conducted technical and business exchanges with companies in the same industry to find new demands and deficiencies in our products.

Finally, we'd like to have a few words on the middle-end. We believe the middle-end is merely a result of step-by-step development. We shall not develop it for its own sake. Our current systems are small applications that are split according to the needs of the business operations. The applications are communicated by way of service invocation, authorized by the unified authentication center. Our current structure is generally termed in the industry as a "micro-service," which is common among internet companies. As business platforms increase, it is necessary to precipitate some core businesses in the form of shared service centers to increase

the reusability so as to form integrated capacity platforms, i.e., the middle-end. Therefore, the middle-end must take place when the business platforms of a enterprise have reached a certain scale, and the organization of the enterprise is platform-oriented to facilitate the business platforms to precipitate downward. In the end, it will form a virtuous circle in which the front-end constantly adapts to changes and the middle-end keeps being stabilized.

徐振震 Ken Xu	徐振震，技术合伙人，2015年加入施璐德，涉猎技术广泛，开源爱好者，代码洁癖重度患者。 Ken, a technological partner who joined CNOOD in 2015, has a wide range of interests in technologies. He is a lover of open source and a "patient" with severe "code mysophobia."
张 牛 Nick Zhang	张牛，技术合伙人，2015年加入施璐德，全面负责系统规划、研发和运营，爱阅读、好运动，新晋奶爸一枚。 Nick, a technical partner, joined CNOOD in 2015. He is responsible for system planning, R&D and operation. He loves reading and sports, and he just became a father.

战略伙伴关系
——应对未来业务的最佳解决方案

Strategic Partnership
—Best Solution for Future Businesses

■ Amir Tafti

如果大家关注一下施璐德公司，就会发现这是一家朝气蓬勃的年轻公司。这不仅在于公司成立的时间较短，更体现在我们的员工面貌上。我们每个人都在努力学习更多的知识和积累更多的经验，不断完善自我。

此外，您还会发现，施璐德公司正在尝试甚至在涉足不同的业务领域和项目，而这意味着要面对更多的困难和挑战。

我已在政府和私企工作超过35年，凭借这些专业的工作经验，我很清楚地知道，世界上没有一家公司能够这样神通广大，可以同时涉足多种不同的业务和领域，但我们可以借助一些解决方案来应对这些难题。在这里，我想要向大家介绍其中一种解决方案，它会帮助施璐德做好准备来应对不同领域的业务和项目。

With a look at CNOOD, you will realize this is a young company, not only according to its date of establishment but also based on the workforce, all of whom looking for more knowledge and more experiences to reach better perfection.

You will also find that right now CNOOD is trying to be and have been involved in different fields of businesses and projects, which means more challenges and difficulties.

As a person with more than 35 years of professional work experience in both government and private sectors, I know very well that no company in the world is capable of entering many different businesses and fields simultaneously, but solutions exist. I would like to pull you toward one of these solutions so that we can prepare our CNOOD for businesses and projects in different fields.

一、引言

战略伙伴关系是指双方或多方达成协议，以共同追求相互协定的目标，但同时又保持相互独立性。在外包关系中，当各方希望达到共同的成果并愿意在该成果的基础上实现长期共赢和创新时，就可以将这种关系发展成为战略伙伴关系。这种合作形式介于并购和有机增长之间。战略伙伴关系是两家或更多组织为实现共同利益而达成同盟关系。

合作伙伴可以为战略伙伴关系提供产品、分销渠道、加工能力、项目资金、资本设备、知识、专长或知识产权等各种资源。伙伴关系是一种合作或协作关系，其

1. Introduction

A strategic partnership is an agreement between two or more parties to pursue a set of agreed upon objectives while remaining independent organizations. A strategic partnership can develop in an outsourcing relationship where the parties desire to achieve long-term win-win benefits and innovation based on mutually desired outcomes. This form of cooperation lies between mergers and acquisitions and organic growth. Strategic partnership occurs when two or more organizations join together to pursue mutual benefits.

Partners may provide the strategic partnership with resources such as products, distribution channels, manufacturing capability, project funding, capital

目的是实现一种协同效应，以便每一方都能从中获得比单打独斗更多的好处。

二、定义

战略伙伴关系有多种定义方法，但有两种方法更为常见：基于合资企业的战略伙伴关系，和不涉及合资企业的战略伙伴关系。

三、基于合资企业的战略伙伴关系的定义

（1）这种模式是指两家或更多参与方达成协议，以共享资源或知识，进而让所有参与方从中受益。这种方法可以弥补自身资产、能力和经营活动的不足，并从外部参与者（如供应商、客户、竞争对手、不同行业的公司或政府部门）获得所需资源或工艺。

（2）这种模式会形成一种组织和法定结构，在该结构内，"合作伙伴"愿意（其实是在利益的激励下愿意）共同行动，共享核心实力。这种模式在战略外包关系中尤为常见。

equipment, knowledge, expertise or intellectual property. The partnership is cooperation or collaboration which aims for a synergy where each partner hopes that the benefits from the partnership will be greater than those from individual efforts.

2. Definitions

There are several ways of defining a strategic partnership, but two methods are more common: strategic partnership based on the joint ventures and strategic partnership excluding joint ventures.

3. Definitions of strategic partnership based on the joint ventures

(1) This model is an agreement between two or more players to share resources or knowledge to be beneficial to all parties involved. It is a way to supplement internal assets, capabilities and activities and get access to the needed resources or techniques from outside players such as suppliers, customers, competitors, companies in different industries or divisions of the government.

(2) On the other hand, this model is an organizational and legal construct wherein "partners" are willing—in fact, motivated—to act in concert and share core competencies. This is especially relevant in strategic outsourcing relationships.

四、不涉及合资企业的战略伙伴关系的定义

（1）两家企业达成协议并决定共享资源，以完成某个对双方都有利的具体项目。与合资企业模式相比（通常两家企业会共同投入资源并创建一个独立的业务实体），这种战略伙伴关系的参与度和持久性都较低。这种模式可以帮助企业开发出更高效的生产工艺、进军新的市场，或者掌控领先竞争对手的优势等。

（2）两家或多家独立公司会达成协议，并为实现共同目标而相互合作。与合资企业不同的是，这种战略伙伴关系中的企业不会成立一家新公司来实现其共同目标，而是在相互协作的同时保持各自的独立性和独特性。

五、按目的划分的战略伙伴关系类型

（1）技术开发伙伴关系。合作各方都希望改进技术和提高专有知识水平，如可能会合并研发部门；达成共同开展工程设计的协议、技术商业化协议以及许可协议或联合开发协议。

（2）运营和物流伙伴关系。合作伙伴共同承担建造新制造设施或生产设施

4. Definitions of strategic partnership excluding joint ventures

(1) An arrangement between two companies that have decided to share resources to undertake a specific, mutually beneficial project. A strategic partnership is less involved and less permanent than a joint venture in which two companies typically pool resources to create a separate business entity. This model could help a company develop a more effective process, expand into a new market or develop an advantage over a competitor, among other possibilities.

(2) Agreement for cooperation among two or more independent firms to work together toward common objectives. Unlike in a joint venture, firms in a strategic partnership do not form a new entity to further their aims but collaborate while remaining apart and distinct.

5. Types of strategic partnership according to the purposes

(1) Technology development partnership: partners with the purpose of improvement in technology and know-how. Examples are consolidated research and development departments, agreements about simultaneous engineering, technology commercialization agreements and licensing or joint development agreements.

(2) Operations and logistics partnership: partners either share the costs

的成本，或利用当地公司在国外的既有基础设施。

（3）市场营销、销售和服务战略伙伴关系。企业利用合作伙伴在国外市场的现有营销和分销基础设施来经销自己的产品，从而更易于进入这些市场。

六、按模式划分的战略伙伴关系类型

（1）许可：一家公司付费使用另一家公司的技术或生产工艺。

（2）行业标准组织：此类组织通常由大型企业组成，并试图根据自身的生产工艺强制推行技术标准。

of implementing new manufacturing or production facilities or utilize already existing infrastructure in foreign countries owned by a local company.

(3) Marketing, sales and service strategic partnership: companies take advantage of the existing marketing and distribution infrastructure of another enterprise in a foreign market to distribute its own products to get easier access to these markets.

6. Types of strategic partnership according to the models

(1) Licensing: A company pays for the right to use another company's technology or production processes.

(2) Industry standard groups: These are groups of normally large enterprises that try to enforce technical standards according to their own production processes.

（3）外包：公司可能会把核心竞争力以外的生产工序外包，这意味着另一家公司会有偿完成这些任务。

（4）联属营销：联属营销是一种基于网络的经销方法，其中一个合作伙伴按照事先确定的条款，通过其销售渠道为合作伙伴提供产品销售机遇。

七、战略伙伴关系的目标

（1）一站式解决方案；
（2）灵活性；
（3）获取新客户；
（4）增强优势，减少弱势；
（5）打开新市场和获取新技术；
（6）资源共享；
（7）共担风险。

八、优势

企业达成战略伙伴关系的优势有多种。

（1）共担风险：伙伴关系可以让其他参与公司帮助自己抵消市场风险。如果参与企业的投资组合能够相互补充，又不构成直接竞争，则战略伙伴关系或可发挥最佳效果。

（2）知识共享：共享技能（经销、营销和管理）、品牌、市场知识、技术专业知识和资产可产生协同效应，这可形成资源池，实现"1+1>2"的效果。

(3) Outsourcing: Production steps that do not belong to the core competencies of a firm are likely to be outsourced, which means that another company is paid to accomplish these tasks.

(4) Affiliate marketing: Affiliate marketing is a web-based distribution method where one partner provides the possibility of selling products via its sales channels in exchange for a beforehand defined provision.

7. Goals of strategic partnership

(1) All-in-one solution;
(2) Flexibility;
(3) Acquisition of new customers;
(4) Add strengths and reduce weaknesses;
(5) Access to new markets and technologies;
(6) Common sources;
(7) Shared risk.

8. Advantages

For companies, there are many reasons to enter a strategic partnership.

(1) Shared risk: A partnership allows the involved companies to offset their market exposure. A strategic partnership probably works best if the companies' portfolio complement each other but do not directly compete.

(2) Shared knowledge: Sharing skills (distribution, marketing and management), brands, market knowledge, technical know-how and assets leads to synergistic effects, which result in a pool of resources which

（3）增长机遇：利用合作伙伴的经销网络，结合良好的品牌形象，可以帮助公司实现比单枪匹马更快的发展速度。

（4）上市速度：在当今竞争激烈的市场上，产品上市速度可决定企业成败，而得力的合作伙伴可以帮助企业显著提高上市速度。

（5）复杂性：随着业务复杂性的增加，企业变得越来越难以满足所有需求以及应对所有挑战，因此集中专业技术和知识资源有助于为客户提供更出色的服务。

（6）创新：伙伴关系中的各方可以一起确定大家共同期望的结果，并制定出包含有助于刺激创新投资的各种激励措施的协议。

（7）成本：伙伴关系有助于降低成本，尤其是在研发等非营利领域。

（8）资源获取：战略伙伴关系中的合作伙伴可以通过提供资源（人力、资金、技术）相互帮助，从而使合作伙伴能够制造出质量更高或成本更低的产品。

（9）进入目标市场：有时，企业必须要与当地伙伴合作才能进入特定的市场。这一点在发展中国家尤其突出，这些国家可能为了保护资源，而极力阻碍外国企业

is more valuable than the separated single resources in the particular companies.

(3) Opportunities for growth: Using the partner's distribution networks in combination with taking advantage of a good brand image can help a company grow faster than it would on its own.

(4) Speed to market: Speed to market is an essential success factor in today's competitive markets, and the right partner can help to distinctly improve this.

(5) Complexity: As complexity increases, it is more and more difficult to manage all the requirements and challenges a company has to face, so pooling of expertise and knowledge can help to best serve customers.

(6) Innovation: The parties in a partnership can jointly determine their mutually desired outcomes and craft a collaborative contract that features incentives designed to spur investments in innovation.

(7) Costs: Partnerships can help to lower costs, especially in non-profit areas like research and development.

(8) Access to resources: Partners in a strategic partnership can help each other by giving access to resources (personnel, finances, technology), which enables the partners to produce their products with a higher quality or in a more cost efficient way.

(9) Access to target markets: Sometimes, collaboration with a local partner is the only way to enter a specific market. Especially, developing countries often

进入市场。

九、缺点

这种伙伴关系虽然有诸多优点，但也存在一些缺点。

（1）共享：在战略伙伴关系中，伙伴必须共享资源和利润，通常还必须共享技能和专业知识。如果这些知识中涉及商业秘密，共享就会有风险。

（2）形成竞争对手：战略伙伴关系中的合作伙伴如果在合作关系中汲取了足够力量，则有一天可能会中止合作关系并成长为竞争对手，然后在同一细分市场上相互竞争。

（3）机会成本：要实现成功的战略伙伴关系，参与企业必须要保证专注并不遗余力，而这可能会阻碍企业抓住对自己有利的其他机会。

（4）不对等的伙伴关系：如果决策权分配极度失衡，弱势一方可能被迫按照强势一方的意愿行事，而违背自身意愿。

（5）国外政府罚没：在境外经营的企业可能面临国外政府取缔其在当地的业务，进而让本土公司占领市场。

want to avoid their resources being exploited, which makes it hard for foreign companies to enter these markets alone.

9. Disadvantages

Although this kind of partnership have many advantages, it also has some disadvantages.

(1) Sharing: In a strategic partnership, the partners must share resources, profits and often skills and know-how. This can be critical if business secrets are included in such knowledge.

(2) Creating a competitor: The partner in a strategic partnership might become a competitor one day if it profits enough from the partnership, grows enough to end the partnership and then is able to operate on its own in the same market segment.

(3) Opportunity costs: Focusing and committing is necessary to run a strategic partnership successfully, but this might discourage the company from taking other opportunities which might be beneficial as well.

(4) Uneven partnership: When the decision power is distributed very unevenly, the weaker partner might be forced to act according to the will of the more powerful partners even if it is actually not willing to do so.

(5) Foreign confiscation: If a company is engaged in a foreign country, there is the risk that the government of this country might try to seize this local business so that

（6）专有信息失控风险：该风险在一些需要广泛协调和密集信息共享的复杂业务中尤其突出。

十、结论（战略伙伴关系的重要性）

对于很多市场和行业来说，建立战略伙伴关系已从可选方案变为必要手段。市场和需求的变化迫使企业建立更多的战略伙伴关系。将战略伙伴关系管理纳入企业的整体战略，对于提升产品和服务水平、打开新市场、获取技术和促进研发具有至关重要的意义。

如今，跨国公司在国内市场以及全球市场都有很多合作伙伴，有时甚至会与竞争对手结盟，这会带来诸多挑战。比如，如何在与合作伙伴保持竞争的同时保护自身利益。

the domestic company can have all the market to its own.

(6) Risk of losing control over proprietary information: This risk is high especially regarding complex transactions requiring extensive coordination and intensive information sharing.

10. Conclusion (importance of strategic partnership)

Strategic partnerships have developed from options to necessities in many markets and industries. Variations in markets and requirements leads to an increasing use of strategic partnerships. It is of essential importance to integrate strategic partnership management into the overall corporate strategy to advance products and services, enter new markets and leverage technology and research and development.

Nowadays, global companies have many partners on inland markets as well as global markets. Sometimes they even partner with competitors, which leads to challenges such as keeping up competition

正如前面所说，施璐德是一家拥有远大前程的年轻公司，所以，我们希望能够为公司找到最佳解决方案，以做好准备来应对不同领域的业务和项目。

让我们不断学习和积累经验，为美好的未来做好准备。

or protecting their own interests while managing the partnerships.

As I mentioned at first, CNOOD is a young company, but with a bright future. So I hope we can find the best solutions for CNOOD, which will make it ready for future businesses and projects in different fields.

Keep learning, collect the experiences, and be ready for the bright future.

Amir Tafti

我叫 Amir Tafti。飞行器工程本科毕业后，我在不同行业领域的政府部门和私营企业工作过，拥有超过 30 年的专业经验，尤其是在工业领域。回首往昔，有好几个理由让我相信自己是一个幸运的人。主要的一个理由是：我在同一个政府机构工作了 20 年，负责对我们国家不同的项目进行审计。我的第一份工作就是在政府部门，工作期间，我从一名普通的职员升为最高级别的经理。我学到了很多东西，并得以积累大量相关经验。此后，私营行业领域同样也为我提供了一个良好的、充满挑战的平台，使我能够成长为合格人才。

现在我已经 56 岁了，很荣幸成为施璐德团队的一员。我将尽我所能，把我的经验和知识传授给同事们，帮助营造一个更好的竞争环境。

I am Amir Tafti, with a Bachelor of Science degree in aircraft engineering and more than 30 years of special work experience in different sectors (especially in industrial fields) in both the government and the private sector. When I look back on my past, I find myself to be a lucky person in many ways. First of all, I worked for 20 years in one special governmental office, responsible for auditing the different projects in my country. It was my first and last governmental job. I started as a common employee and ended up as a top-level manger, I learned a lot and collected a huge amount of related experience. After that, even the private sector I worked in provided a good and challengeable platform for me to grow to be qualified person.

Now 56 years old, it is my pleasure to join the CNOOD team and do my best to transfer my experience and knowledge to my colleagues to create a better competitive environment.

2019年，我与施璐德不平凡的一年

2019, A Marvelous Year for Me and CNOOD

■ Wenxin Huang

最近看过的一本书中的研究表示，如果一个企业或者团队太稳定，尽管按部就班，但不容易产生创新和变化，所以这就需要一些外来合作者参与。作为施璐德的合作伙伴，我和施璐德结识有6年多了，希望能够以旁观者角度，为施璐德多给点建议，多做点实在事情，如书上所说给这个团队带来一些好的变化。

2019年真是不平凡的一年，年底出现的新冠肺炎疫情仍在延续（截至2020年3月）。

2019年初，施璐德意气风发地计划了很多大动作，包括本溪的投资、湖南公司的设立、新西兰业务的开拓，以及有色矿产的进口等。可以说，这些都有我直接、

I recently read a book claiming that when a business or a team is immersed in steady operations, following procedures and prescribing orders for too long, it will unlikely generate innovation and changes. At this moment, some outsiders are called for to stir the waters. As a partner of CNOOD, I have been acquainted with the company for over six years. From the view of a bystander, I'd like to give some advice and do something real to make a difference in CNOOD, that is, to bring some changes in the right direction for this organization as the book suggests.

The year 2019 was an extraordinary one. The COVID-19 epidemic broke out and extended into 2020 (up to March, 2020).

In early 2019, I noticed that CNOOD made big moves in high feather. It invested in Benxi, established a branch in Hunan Province, expanded its business to

间接地参与，正是因为我会参与，所以我也非常乐观，意气风发起来，感觉2019年可以大有作为一番。

回顾2019年，施璐德的业务的确有很大增长，但是美中不足，同样很多业务非常可惜地没有顺利开展起来，包括上面提到的一些项目。我在2020年春节期间有过反思与总结：是老池的判断错误了吗？是老池盲目乐观了吗？

我还记得2019年春节前出差去长沙，因为一个话题，老池提醒我，要耐住性子（做事）！经过这个春节的反思，我想说，从我了解到的信息，老池当初当机立断做的决定并不是鲁莽的。本溪是个好投资机会，2019年国内的融资去杠杆过度，国务院在2020年也做了纠正；包括湖南公司的设立，还有有色矿产的进口，很多机会是关联的，想要打入新的领域，都会遇到万事开头难。比如，国内大型铜企都找到我们了，最后还是没有促成合作。新西兰的业务方向是好的，但同样地，必然要广泛撒网，才可能有收获，不可能一招即中。

New Zealand and imported nonferrous minerals. I was involved, directly or indirectly, in all of these moves. Because of my involvement, I turned optimistic and spirited, feeling that I could accomplish much in 2019.

Now as we look back on 2019, CNOOD has broadened its business quite a lot, but it has also left much to be desired and has failed to advance many operations, including the ones mentioned above. I pondered over it during the Spring Festival, wondering if Dennis misjudged the market and was blinded with optimism.

I still remember my business trip to the city of Changsha before the Spring Festival of 2019. I chatted with Dennis. He reminded me to be patient at work! As I contemplated it during this Spring Festival, I would say that from what I've learned, Dennis was not reckless in making his prompt decisions at that time. Benxi proved a good investment opportunity. In 2019, China launched excessive financing deleveraging, which has been corrected by the State Council this year. Many opportunities, such as the Hunan project and the import of nonferrous minerals, were closely associated. It's hard to begin as we gain entry into the new field. Even China's copper giant approached us, though we did not reach a deal in the end. The New Zealand business was a step in the right direction, although by the same token, it calls for casting the net widely to have a

虽然回头看,老池的这些决定似乎没有收成,也在两个海外项目上付了一些"学费"。但是,同样地,没有老池的一些决定,恐怕也不会有2019年施璐德的业绩大发展。

我心里感慨的是,怎样作为旁观者,给点建议,或者做些什么,更大限度地让施璐德发挥出优势,限制劣势对决策的干扰。当然不是说,要从风险角度来阻止老池去做一些决定,这样可能扼杀了创造力,企业就再也停滞不前了,好的机会也就错过了。就和炒股票一样,希望为施璐德提供止损措施,任何决策不能只计算顺利成功的结果,在最坏情况下,止损措施可以保护到施璐德。老池还是理性的,反复提醒过我们,现在是多事之秋,从中美贸易摩擦,到各国贸易保护主义,再到疫情对出口企业复工的影响,已然演变为全球疫情的风险提升。我想说,中国借助20年的出口红利,轻松赚钱的日子已经一去不复返了。用现在专家的话说,在信息高度透明的背景下,现在的红利是苟且红利。你只有不苟且做事,多用心,更专注,那做事苟且的企业会被淘汰,你才能不依靠苟且做事,获得红利。想想2019年初的意气风发,我们做事是否有过苟且的地方呢?如果是,自然会给你教训;2020年,做事不苟且,相信会有好的回报。希望把这点心得送给施璐德大家庭,不能仅仅老池一个人不苟且,需要所有人不苟且,勉励各位!

good harvest. We can't hit right on the nail just with one move.

Now looking back, Dennis' decisions seem to be fruitless, and the company paid some tuition fees and learned its lessons on two overseas projects. However, without some of his decisions, there would not have been the big boost in CNOOD performance in 2019.

As an external aide, I'm thinking about how I can offer some advice or do something to help bring the advantages of CNOOD into display while playing down the disadvantages that interfere with decision-making. Surely, I will not dissuade Dennis from making decisions from the perspective of the risks involved, as this would stifle creativity. Business growth would come to a halt, and good opportunities would be missed. Just as in stock market speculation, I hope Dennis could work out measures to stop losses. We should not make decisions that only consider successful results. Instead, we should come up with answers for the worst scenario, in which we may stop losses and protect CNOOD. Dennis is a rational man nonetheless. He has been alerting us that this is an eventful year, ranging from the China-U.S. trade frictions to protectionism in various countries, as well as the impact of the COVID-19 epidemic on work resumption in export-oriented enterprises, which has evolved into an increasingly risky global pandemic. The days of making easy money by virtue of the two-decade-long export dividends are gone. As experts put it, the dividends today are perfunctory ones due to the high transparency of information. Only when we work earnestly, diligently and attentively will we earn the dividends while seeing the elimination of those that muddle along. Now, as we reflect on our high spirits in early 2019, did we resign to circumstances once in a while? If so, we would be taught a lesson. In the new year, since we work diligently, we are confident of good returns. Here, I share my perception to all CNOOD members in the hope that everyone works hard along with Dennis.

黄文欣
Wenxin Huang

毕业于上海大学（本科），曾就职于兴业银行上海分行，现就职于中国出口信用保险公司上海分公司。

Wenxin graduated from Shanghai University and used to work for the Shanghai branch of Industrial Bank. Currently, he works for the Shanghai branch of China Export & Credit Insurance Corporation (Sinosure).

未来·即来
The Future Is Coming

■ Neo Wu

2019年,
我当爸爸了,生了个可爱的女儿。

她出生那天,我从护士手中接过来,看到她的第一眼,有点慌,感觉不太真实,我居然当爸爸了。

现在她每天慢慢地长大,已经会爬,喜欢咿咿呀呀地叫,还会挤眉弄眼,喜欢抢手机,爱撕书,听到有节奏的音乐会摇头晃脑,有点皮,不经意间会叫声爸爸、妈妈;她妈妈说什么都像我,睡觉打呼、流口水,不喜欢洗脸、涂霜。

我也渐渐习惯了有她的存在,下班早点回到家抱抱她,陪她看看书。

将来,她长大了,希望她没有太多的纠结,享受生活。

In 2019,

I became a father and now have a lovely daughter.

The day she was born, I took her from the nurse and felt a bit confused at the first sight of her. It seemed hardly true that I had actually become a father.

She is growing up every day, able to crawl, fond of babbling and winking now and then. She likes playing cell phones and tearing up books. She would wag her head naughtily when hearing rhythmic music. She would call Dad and Mom by accident. Her mom said she was like me in every way, snoring and drooling in sleep and hating washing face and applying cream.

I'm getting used to having her. After work, I would go home earlier, hug her and read books for her.

I hope that in the future, when she grows up, she will enjoy her life without

2020年，
一切都在变。
原来为人子，现在为人父；初到公司的样子，现在的样子；2019年初的样子，2020年初的样子。

2020年，新冠肺炎疫情在全球蔓延，石油价格的暴跌，着实打乱了世界前进的脚步。

供应商，受疫情的影响，生产效率降低，不确定性增加，因国内市场井喷，生产成本升高，导致我们采购成本增加。

much to struggle with.

In 2020,
Everything is changing.
Previously, I was only a son, but now I am also a father. I looked that way when I first came to the company, and I look like this now. I looked that way in early 2019, and I look like this now in early 2020.

In 2020, the spread of the COVID-19 epidemic and the sharp drop in oil prices have indeed disrupted the pace of the world.

Due to the impact of the pandemic, the suppliers become less productive. With more uncertainties, blowout in the domestic market and rising production costs, the purchasing costs will increase as well.

客户，因国外疫情的暴发，不确定性增加，项目出现暂停、延期，甚至取消；唯一庆幸的是，公司早有远见，只做工程项目。工程项目意味着，周期长、投资大，非逼不得已，业主不会也不敢轻易变动计划，项目还得继续。反观服装、日用品外贸行业，订单被取消已比比皆是。

货运，因为疫情，国外封港，要求船舶检疫，不确定性大大增加。

所以，当下对于项目能否安全顺利执行的考量，要远大于对项目利润率的评估。

基于以上的原因，加之后来的国际关系紧张，以后国际贸易的日形势会更难。

都说2019年是过去十年最差的一年，却是未来十年最好的一年；2019年确实比2020年好一些。

对我们而言，只做工程项目，供的是产品，同时也是服务。只有依靠我们的资源整合、我们和工厂的良好关系、我们的口碑、我们对质量的态度、我们在工厂的坚守、我们和客户的相互信任，客户才与我们合作，而工厂一直都在那里。

Following the spread of the pandemic and the increase in uncertainty worldwide, many projects are suspended, postponed or even canceled. Fortunately, CNOOD has long been far-sighted. It takes only engineering projects, which mean long periods and big investments. Unless by absolute necessity, the project owners will not and dare not change their plans rashly. The projects will continue. In contrast, a great many foreign trade orders of clothes and daily necessities have been canceled.

Due to the global pandemic, many foreign harbors have been locked, and ship quarantine inspections have become stricter. The uncertainty of freight transport has increased dramatically.

Therefore, smooth implementation of projects have outweighed the profit margins.

Taking all these elements into account, as well as the tensions in international relations that followed, the international trade will meet harder days ahead.

It has been acknowledged that 2019 was the worst year in the past decade. But it may be the best year in the next decade. The year 2019 was indeed a little bit better than 2020.

We are engaged only in engineering projects. We supply products and services. Depending on our resource integration, we have kept good relations with factories. Because of our reputation, our attention to quality, our persistence in factories and

戴森很贵，但是一直都有人愿意买，是因为其品质有保障，好的服务才会带来品牌的溢价。其他品牌，同样的产品，谁又愿意去花那个钱呢？

未来时局艰难，我们需要放慢脚步，压缩非必要的成本，大家一心、稳扎稳打、共同努力。

our mutual trust with customers, we have firmed up cooperation with customers, though the factories have always been there.

Dyson is expensive, but it has many loyal buyers because it has guaranteed quality, sound service and brand premium. Who would spend the same money on the same products of another brand?

Tough times lie ahead. We have to slow down and reduce unnecessary costs. Let's unite as one to forge ahead steadily and surely.

吴珍荣
Neo Wu

出生于福建南平，2008 年毕业于上海海事大学，两年远洋航海工作经历；2014 年有幸加入 CNOOD 并工作至今。

Neo was born in Nanping, Fujian Province. He graduated from Shanghai Maritime University in 2008 and had two years' working experience of ocean shipping. He joined CNOOD in 2014.

海外施工感触

My Overseas Construction Experiences

■ Peter Tao & Thompson Lee

网上看到一篇文章，分析传统国内承包商承接海外项目的特点，即"中国设计+中国制造+中国施工、安装、调试"模式，具体如下：

（1）投标及执行阶段，无论是设计院方案、数据表，还是施工、安装等单位做的项目文件，都与欧美业主要求存在一定差距。

（2）使用的设备优先采用中国制造的产品。

（3）项目的工期短，但项目建设的过

I read an article on the Internet that summed up the traditional characteristics of Chinese contractors undertaking overseas projects. By following the pattern of Chinese design, Chinese manufacturing, as well as Chinese construction, installation and commissioning, they present the following features:

A. At the bidding and contract implementation stage, Chinese contractors still have some way to go to meet the requirements of European and American project developers in the preparation of programs and data sheets by design institutes and the preparation project files by construction and installation companies.

B. Chinese contractors prefer to adopt China-made products when it comes to the selection of equipment for projects.

C. Chinese contractors can complete

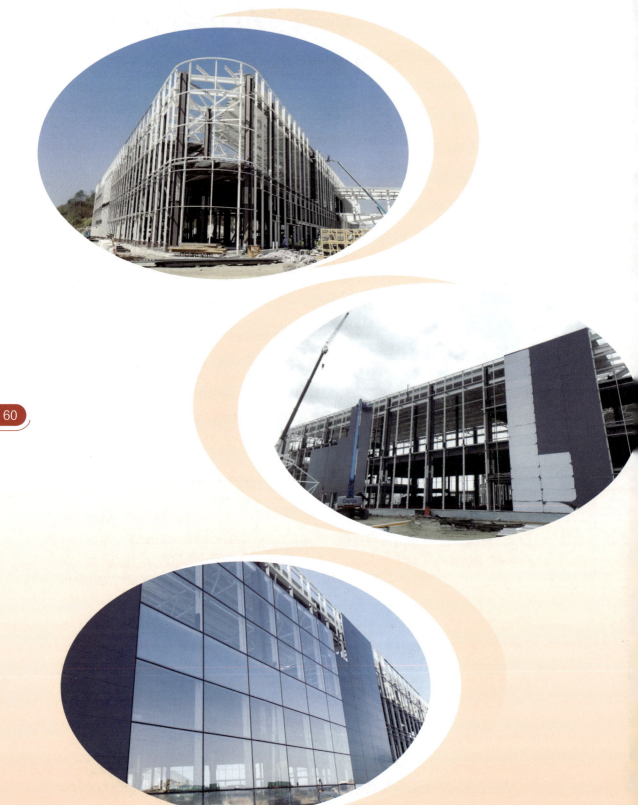

程管理较差；关注项目的建设移交，而轻视过程中的质量保证和文件资料。

（4）各相关方仅仅在中国规范下封闭运行时比较顺畅，对外国标准则不适应。

（5）对合同的签订和管理不严格，当发生纠纷时，受中国传统文化的影响倾向于通过领导沟通和上级单位协调来解决。

（6）对于跨文化的沟通障碍不够重视，不善于融入对方的社会等。

作为常年参与海外项目的一分子，看到这种分析，感触颇深，我们总是力图在参与的项目中尽力规避这种种的不足。

巴拿马Amador项目作为完全按照美国钢结构协会AISC抗震和焊接规范、美国建筑制造商协会AAMA幕墙规范进行设计、制作和安装的海外项目，CNOOD需要按照美标完成相关钢管桩、钢结构、金属幕墙、金属楼承板、金属夹芯屋面的优化设计、深化、加工和现场安装工作。我们规避了传统国内承包商在海外项目实施过程中的一些问题。一路走来，项目的顺利推进，离不开项目团队各位成员的齐心协力和辛勤付出。

a project fast, but they are poor in process management. They stress project construction and transfer but often neglect quality guarantee and documentation in the process.

D. The parties concerned have smooth operation in closed circumstances under Chinese standards, but they are maladjusted to foreign standards.

E. Chinese contractors are less strict in contract signing and management. In case of disputes, they are inclined to solve them through leadership communication and coordination of the superior units due to the influence of Chinese traditional culture.

F. Chinese contractors have not paid sufficient attention to the barriers of cross-cultural communication, so they are not good at melting into the local society.

As a man engaged in overseas projects all year round, I'm deeply touched when reading this article. As far as we are concerned, we have racked our brains to avoid such deficiencies in our projects.

For instance, the Panama Amador project is an overseas project of ours that is designed, constructed and installed fully in compliance with the American Institute of Steel Construction (AISC) seismic and welding specifications and the American Architectural Manufacturers Association (AAMA) curtain wall specifications. We are required to complete the optimized design, development, processing and on-site installation of the steel pipe piles, steel structures, metal curtain walls, metal

floor bearing plates and metal sandwich roofs in accordance with the American standards. In this process, we have avoided the problems met by traditional Chinese contractors in implementing overseas projects. To date, we are advancing the project smoothly, which is inseparable from the concerted efforts and hard work of all members of our project team.

在整个设计和深化阶段，运用了SAP2000、RISA Connection、L-pile、Tekla Structure 等多种设计软件，整合了地勘、基础、结构、建筑相关设计资料，按照相关美标，历时近 4 个月完成了设计优化和详图深化报批工作。

In the design and development stage, we applied multiple design software, such as SAP2000, RISA Connection, L-pile and Tekla Structure, to integrate design data relating to geological exploration, infrastructure, structure and building. We spent nearly four months to complete the design optimization and detailed drawing improvement for approval under relevant US standards.

在加工制作阶段，项目组基于公司 Workbench 平台，历时近 6 个月出色完成了钢管桩、钢结构、金属夹芯墙板、铝合金玻璃幕墙、金属楼承板、金属夹芯屋面板、钢拉杆、高强螺栓及各种施工用杂配件的生产、采购、催交、质控、物流工作。

作为项目实施关键节点的现场施工环节，项目组面对如下挑战：

（1）所有施工方案均用西班牙语报批，经业主咨询公司批准后，项目组方可进场施工，现场安全文明施工要求高，施工验收标准严。

（2）初进场施工，巴拿马正值雨季，每天几乎都有 3～4 小时的雷阵雨，当地法规要求下雨期间必须停工，面对进度压力，大家不得不望"雨"兴叹。非雨季气温则高达 36～40℃，为典型热带炎热气候。

In the processing and production stage, our project team spent nearly six months to excellently complete the production, procurement, delivery, quality control and logistics of steel pipe piles, steel structures, metal sandwich wall panels, aluminum alloy glass curtain walls, metal floor bearing plates, metal sandwich roofs, steel tension bars, high-strength bolts and various miscellaneous parts for the construction. They were performed on the company's Workbench platform.

Our project team, which is responsible for site construction, a key link to complete the project, have faced the following challenges:

A. All the construction plans were submitted to the authorities for approval in Spanish. We should first win approval of the project developer to enter the site for construction. The project developer has placed high standards on safety during field work and is strict in the acceptance check.

B. As we first entered the site for construction, it happened to be the rainy season in Panama. Thundershowers would last for three to four hours almost every day. According to the local law, we had to suspend work to take shelter from rain. Despite heavy schedule pressure, we had to lament our littleness before the downpours. When the rainy season is gone, the temperature would soar up to 36~40℃, a result of the typical tropical hot climate.

（3）由于现场临近太平洋，海风很大，在进行安装屋面板和幕墙面板的高空作业时，对安全保障工作的要求极高。

（4）海边高温高盐环境气候对钢构件、杂配件的堆存提出了更高的要求，如何防止钢构件、杂配件的快速锈蚀和损坏就成了摆在大家面前的一道难题。

（5）在场地有限的情况下，总计300多个集装箱货物在施工现场的卸货、摆放和保护，显得尤为棘手。

（6）当地劳动力效率和熟练程度堪忧，刚开始安装，甚至没有对准钢柱中心线和地脚锚栓中心线的经验，钢柱的垂直度仅使用线锤就认为可以达到标准。进度压力再大，当地工人到点就会收拾工具下班，有时甚至需要亲自盯住吊车司机，怕他们提前下班。

C. Since our construction site sits near the Pacific Ocean, gale howls from the sea. Hence, we have to be particular about the safety guarantee in work high above the ground such as the installation of roof panels and curtain wall panels.

D. At the seaside, the high-temperature and high-salt environment have placed higher requirements on the storage of steel components and miscellaneous fittings. We have to meet the challenge of the fast rusting and damage of the steel components and miscellaneous fittings.

E. It is a knotty problem to unload, store and protect cargoes of over 300 containers with the limited space at the construction site.

We are upset at the low efficiency and proficiency of the local labor force. As we started to install the facilities, they didn't even have the experience of aligning the steel centerlines and anchor bolt centerlines. They believed they could meet the standard by merely employing a plumb line to measure the perpendicularity of a steel column. Despite the schedule pressure, they would pick up the tools and leave at the quitting time. Sometimes, we had to keep a close watch on the crane drivers, in case they would get off work earlier.

（7）施工现场管理的复杂性，从11月中旬到12月下旬，最多有80多名当地工人和40多名中国工人，分白班和夜班在现场不间断作业，涉及不同区域、不同工序、不同利益相关方，这要求现场管理人员具备出色的沟通能力、管理能力和面对突发事件的反应处理能力。

（8）施工用吊装机械、登高车故障率较高，报修后影响继续施工；应急的小型机具经常需要在当地紧急采购，价格是国内的数倍。

（9）后勤保障要求高，近50人的项目团队的衣食住行保障工作量大。

面对这些困难，大家坚守现场，早出晚归，群策群力，团结一致，始终把项目履约放在第一位；越是条件艰苦越是干劲十足，最直观的就是大家肤色都增加了几个色度，从黄色变成了黝黑色。

目前，项目总体进入收尾阶段，项目团队也会再接再厉，确保项目实体顺利交工。我们觉得做海外项目如果仅仅想着签约、生效、完成和收汇，那得到的仅仅是数字和报表，这些或许会让你升职加薪，但时间越久你越不会感到事业感和成就

G. It is fairly complex in construction site management. In the peak period from mid November to late December, we had over 80 local workers and 40 Chinese workers operating simultaneously on the site in day and night shifts, involving diversified quarters, working procedures and stakeholders. This required the site administrators to have excellent communication skills, management ability, and quick response to emergencies.

H. The hoisting machinery and elevators had a high failure rate. The repair affected continuous construction. We had to buy small machines and tools from the local market to meet emergencies, although they were quoted at prices several times higher than those in China.

I. The logistics support was a demanding task, as it was to provide basic necessities of life for nearly 50 staff workers on the project team.

In the face of all these difficulties, we have stood fast on the site, going out early and returning late. We have pooled the wisdom and efforts of everyone, united as one, and put it in the first place to honor the contract. We remain energetic despite the hard conditions. So far, we have all been tanned, looking from yellow to pitch-dark at a glance.

Now the project is winding up. We will work even harder to ensure smooth delivery of the project. In my opinion, if we were concerned only with signing contracts, bringing them into effect, completing them and

感。只有对这个国家的喜怒哀乐、人文脉搏、民族脾性有了感情，它的进步、它的发展中都有我们的贡献，这才会让人觉得一切付出都有了完全不同的意义。

taking the money, we would reap only numbers and statements in overseas projects. These achievements may help us win promotion and get rich, but the longer we are involved, the less sense of accompanishment we will feel in our career. Only when we are emotionally attached to the country, its culture and national character and witness our efforts have contributed to its progress and dcvclopment will we find that our devotions have an entirely different significance.

陶 涛
Peter Tao

2006年毕业于北京科技大学土木工程专业，曾先后供职于上海宝冶集团有限公司和SGS通标标准技术服务（上海）有限公司，美国石油协会压力容器检验员，沙特阿美认证检验员，国际焊接学会国际焊接工程师，美国焊接协会焊接检验员。拥有10余年技术、项目管理和检验经验，于2017年1月加入施璐德亚洲有限公司。

Peter graduated from University of Science and Technology Beijing majoring in civil engineering. He has worked for Shanghai Baoye Group Corporation and SGS-CSTC Standards Technical Services (Shanghai) Co., Ltd. He is a Pressure Vessel Inspector of the American Petroleum Institute, a Saudi Aramco approved inspector, an International Welding Engineer certified by the International Institute of Welding and a Certified Welding Inspector of American Welding Society. With more than ten years of experience in techniques, project management and inspection, he joined CNOOD Asia Limited in January 2017.

李振宇
Thompson Lee

1992年生，硕士研究生，毕业于上海大学材料工程专业，2016加入施璐德。

Thompson was born in 1992. He graduated from Shanghai University with a master's degree in materials engineering and joined CNOOD in 2016.

写给施璐德所有成员的一首诗
A Poem for All CNOOD's Members

■ Nicolas Kipreos

通往成功的道路要经历重重考验，

所以，你要相信自己，相信施璐德。

心怀远大梦想，让激情闪耀光芒，

否则，那就是自断前程。

挑战现状，并在挑战中成长，

不要忘记，施璐德始终追求无限梦想。

始终精益求精，提高自我，

否则，那就是自断前程。

只要你用头脑思考，聆听内心，

就会在施璐德飞得更高。

公平竞争，爱岗敬业，

否则，那就是自断前程。

The road to success is paved with tests;

Therefore, you have to believe in yourself and in CNOOD.

Dream big, and let your passion shine;

If you do not do it, you are ruining your future.

Challenge the status quo; go further in your challenges,

Remember that CNOOD is an endless quest of opportunities.

Do not forget to always improve for excellence,

If you do not do it, you are ruining your future.

If you think with your head and listen to your heart,

You will fly high in CNOOD.

Play fair and work hard;

If you do not do it, you are ruining your future.

做你热爱的工作，并热爱自己的工作，

这就是在施璐德成功的关键。

Do what you love and love what you do,

This is the key to CNOOD's future.

尼古拉斯
Nicolas Kipreos

尼古拉斯出生于一个希腊裔家庭，当初他们为谋求更好机遇而举家徙居智利时，可谓身无长物，唯有成功之渴望、自由之身心，以及他们的爱心和对天主计划的信德。此后，他与兄弟和两个姐妹在极为清晰的原则指引下长大成人，受到过良好的教育和道德的熏陶，养成了简朴的生活方式，心中充满无尽之爱。几家声誉卓著的机构培养陶冶了他，帮助他实现远大理想。1993年，他与帕特里夏结为伉俪，育有四个儿女，一家人其乐融融。他信仰虔诚，日进日新，对待同事，真诚友善，但对自己认定正确之事抑或更佳之策，则必为之争辩，不轻言放弃。恒守敬人之道，临事唯以信、爱、真。一以贯之者，宽以待人、严以求实。

他不怕犯错，但若因自己未做分内之事、未能恪尽职守而累及他人，则必心怀畏惧。在施璐德，他受到热情欢迎，颇感自在裕如。自觉有义务为公司服务，期待不久即可回报。

他的座右铭是："正面思考，积极主动，充满自信，信仰坚定，生活必将更为稳定，更多实干行动，留下更丰富的经历和成果。"

Nicolas was born to a Greek family who moved to Chile looking for better opportunities. They brought with them nothing but their desire to succeed, their mental and physical freedom, their love, and their faith in God's designs. Thus, he was raised with his brother and two sisters with very clear principles, good education and morals, simplicity in the way of living and infinite love. He was molded in several institutions of great reputation that have allowed him to reach great ideals. He married Patricia in 1993 and has four children, forming a happy family. He lives his faith piously, tries to improve every day and is honest and kind to his colleagues, but he also always defends what he believes to be right or better, never giving up easily. He always treats people with respect and deals with affairs with integrity, love and sincerity. He is always soft on the person and hard on the issue.

He is not afraid of making mistakes, but he feels ashamed if others are affected because he didn't fulfill his responsibilities. He feels very comfortable at CNOOD where he has been generously welcomed. He feels a debt to the company and hopes to pay it off soon.

His maxim is "think positively and actively, with confidence and faith, and life will become more secure, more fraught with actions and richer in experience and achievement."

哪些特点成就了别具特色的施璐德

Which Are the Characteristics That Make CNOOD a Unique Company?

■ Nicolas Kipreos

施璐德是一家蓬勃发展的成功企业，我认为，以下六大特点成就了这家别具特色的公司。

1. 以目的为导向的公司文化

施璐德的员工具有明确的目标意识；明白自己的近期和长期目标。这一点非常重要，因为一家目的明确的企业会合理地调配人力和物力资源来实现目标而不是简单地管理目标。管理目标的终极目的难道不就是实现目标吗？答案是肯定的，要培养具有可持续性、可扩展性的强大公司文化，首先必须具有明确的目标。

目的明确能够激励员工，提高员工的敬业度。我们公司董事长 Dennis 和首席执行官 Fay 在向施璐德员工提出明确目的时，会激励并鼓励员工互动，以提供强大

CNOOD, as successful company, in my opinion manifests six distinct characteristics that makes it a unique company in the world.

1. A purpose–driven company culture

CNOOD's employees have a clear sense of purpose and understand their immediate and long-term goals. This is important because an organization with purpose shifts people and resources forward in order to achieve goals rather than simply managing them, and achieving goals is what it's all about, isn't it? Yes, purpose is a key ingredient for a strong, sustainable, scalable organizational culture.

Purpose is an inspirational driver for engaging employees. When our leaders, Dennis Chi (Chairman) and Fay Lee (CEO), establish a clear purpose

的动力源泉。换言之，组织的战略、实力和文化成为了有效推动公司实现自身目标的引擎。

2. 有效的沟通

在施璐德，有效的沟通具有三大特征：清晰、礼貌和主动。

清晰是决定沟通成败的关键，因为以透明、清晰、简洁的方式传递信息至关重要。施璐德正是通过清楚地传达信息成就了伟大业绩，并让我们的团队拥有强大的战斗力。在我们的组织中，如果员工能够清晰、安全地表达自己的想法，团队就能更好地合作，生产力也会随之提高。

施璐德还非常重视以礼貌的方式开展沟通，这使得员工可在安全和相互尊重的氛围中传递信息。这一点表现为大家相互尊重，并在这种尊重的安全范围内传递信息。各种反馈、信息和消息就是通过这种方式在施璐德传递，以将彼此之间的伤害降到最低。

"主动"是施璐德开展有效沟通的另一个重要方面。我们认为，只有员工主动参与，才能实现富有成效的讨论。我们倡导"着眼未来"的讨论，我们认为往事已

for CNOOD people, they inspire and engage us, providing a concrete source for motivation. In other words, the organization's strategies, capabilities and culture become the engine behind the organization's purpose.

2. Effective communication

Effective communication in CNOOD has three main characteristics: clarity, courtesy and proactivity.

Clarity is a vital element in effective communication because it is important for messages and information to be transferred in a transparent, clear and concise manner. It is the clarity of the messages in CNOOD that allows us to give the maximum and that makes us an invaluable team. In our organization, where employees express themselves clearly and safely, teams work together better, and productivity is increased as a result.

Courtesy is another important aspect of communication in CNOOD. It allows messages to be transmitted within an atmosphere of safety and respect. It manifests respect for the other person and gets the message across within the safe limits of that respect. This way, feedback, information and messages are transferred in CNOOD with minimal concern over getting hurt or hurting others.

Proactivity is yet another crucial aspect of the effective communication in CNOOD. We believe that the only way to conduct a productive discussion is

矣，不可改变，所以在讨论中要更多地关注从现在开始，应该如何达到我们的目标或相互协作以取得更好成绩。

3. 反馈文化

我们认为，反馈是施璐德成功的关键。为什么？因为反馈能够推动绩效提升。创造以反馈为导向的开放企业文化需要员工乐于提出和接受反馈，并知道何时以及如何提出反馈。不管是员工还是客户，都可以提出反馈。反馈可能涉及各个方面，比如领导力和愿景、管理和内部实践以及运营方式等。反馈文化不只是提出和接受反馈，还要在密切注意文化、个性以及情况多样性的前提下，确保能够安全、清晰和切实有效地提出和接受反馈。

4. 拥抱多样性

文化敏感性是指企业文化要意识到与自己不同的实践做法和文化。拥抱多样性的文化，就像施璐德一直所践行的那样，要了解不同的文化，知道如何走近这些不同的文化并与相应的人群交流。我们上海公司的最高管理层一直在评估文化差异会对人们的工作、交流和互动产生怎样的影响，而从不主观地做出判断和假设，从不

to conduct a proactive one. A forward-looking discussion is based on the notion that whatever happened has happened and cannot be changed, so the discussion is more centered on what we can do from this point going forward in order to reach our goals or to operate better as a team.

3. A culture of feedback

In CNOOD, we think that feedback is crucial to the success of our organization. Why? Because feedback pushes the levels of performance higher. Creating an open, feedback-oriented company culture requires people to be receptive to giving and receiving feedback and to understand when and how to give it. Feedback can come from our own employees or customers; it does not matter. The feedback could be about any aspect, including leadership and vision, management and internal practices, and operations. A culture of feedback means not only that feedback is given and received but also that it is given and received safely, clearly and productively, with sensitivity to the diversity of cultures, personalities and situations.

4. Embracing diversity

Cultural sensitivity is the awareness of practices and cultures that are different from your own. A culture that embraces diversity, like the one that CNOOD's follows, has an awareness of different cultures, of how these cultures should be properly approached and of how to communicate with them accordingly. Our

歧视不同文化的人群或对任何人群形成刻板印象。

施璐德拥抱多样性，并将相互包容与海纳百川的精神视作企业的核心文化，为培养团队精神和全面合作提供了沃土。

5. 团队精神

这是施璐德内部的关键文化。创造、增强和倡导团队精神是施璐德文化的核心。一支相互合作的团队所能达到的成就远远高于每个人单打独斗；如果整个团队都能发挥个人专长，集思广益，往往能够拿出更好的解决办法来有效地解决问题。相互支持还有助于鼓励人们成功实现他们可能并未意识到自己可以实现的目标。

6. 成长与发展

施璐德始终通过培训为员工提供成长机会，提升员工的个人能力或团队合作能力。施璐德的管理人员不仅要激励员工发挥最佳表现，同时还要帮助员工不断成长和发展。在施璐德，为员工提供发展机会是提升员工敬业度的决定性手段。

top management in Shanghai is always evaluating how certain cultural differences affect how people work, communicate and interact without judging, making assumptions, discriminating or stereotyping.

CNOOD embraces diversity, and it is centered on tolerance and acceptance of others, which fosters teamwork and a general sense of collaboration.

5. Teamwork

This is key inside CNOOD. Creating, enhancing and celebrating teamwork is at the heart of CNOOD's culture. When a team works well together, as a unit, it is able to accomplish more than its individual members working alone; when members apply different skills, they are often able to come up with a more effective solution than one person working on the same problem alone. Mutual support can have the benefit of encouraging people to achieve goals they may not have realized they could reach on their own.

6. Growth and development

CNOOD's culture is always offering us opportunities for growth, both in terms of training and in terms of the ability to grow as individuals or as teams. It is CNOOD's manager's job to not only obtain the best possible performance from us but also help us grow at the same time. At CNOOD, opportunities for growth are an incredibly determining factor in our engagement.

尼古拉斯
Nicolas Kipreos

尼古拉斯出生于一个希腊裔家庭,当初他们为谋求更好机遇而举家徙居智利时,可谓身无长物,唯有成功之渴望、自由之身心,以及他们的爱心和对天主计划的信德。此后,他与兄弟和两个姐妹在极为清晰的原则指引下长大成人,受到过良好的教育和道德的熏陶,养成了简朴的生活方式,心中充满无尽之爱。几家声誉卓著的机构培养陶冶了他,帮助他实现远大理想。1993年,他与帕特里夏结为伉俪,育有四个儿女,一家人其乐融融。他信仰虔诚,日进日新,对待同事,真诚友善,但对自己认定正确之事抑或更佳之策,则必为之争辩,不轻言放弃。恒守敬人之道,临事唯以信、爱、真。一以贯之者,宽以待人、严以求实。

他不怕犯错,但若因自己未做分内之事、未能恪尽职守而累及他人,则必心怀畏惧。在施璐德,他受到热情欢迎,颇感自在裕如。自觉有义务为公司服务,期待不久即可回报。

他的座右铭是:"正面思考,积极主动,充满自信,信仰坚定,生活必将更为稳定,更多实干行动,留下更丰富的经历和成果。"

Nicolas was born to a Greek family who moved to Chile looking for better opportunities. They brought with them nothing but their desire to succeed, their mental and physical freedom, their love, and their faith in God's designs. Thus, he was raised with his brother and two sisters with very clear principles, good education and morals, simplicity in the way of living and infinite love. He was molded in several institutions of great reputation that have allowed him to reach great ideals. He married Patricia in 1993 and has four children, forming a happy family. He lives his faith piously, tries to improve every day and is honest and kind to his colleagues, but he also always defends what he believes to be right or better, never giving up easily. He always treats people with respect and deals with affairs with integrity, love and sincerity. He is always soft on the person and hard on the issue.

He is not afraid of making mistakes, but he feels ashamed if others are affected because he didn't fulfill his responsibilities. He feels very comfortable at CNOOD where he has been generously welcomed. He feels a debt to the company and hopes to pay it off soon.

His maxim is "think positively and actively, with confidence and faith, and life will become more secure, more fraught with actions and richer in experience and achievement."

与正能量光芒的人同行

Advancing in the Company of Men with Positive Energy

■ Tina Jiang

俗话说：行要有好伴，居要有好邻。

人活在世上，和谁在一起很重要，和什么样的人在一起，可能就会有什么样的人生。你和谁在一起，就会成为什么样的人。和优秀的人在一起，勇敢地向上生长，你才会站在不一样的高度，看到不一样的风景。

我的身边就有一群靠谱的、有正能量的人。所谓靠谱，就是凡事有交代，件件有着落，事事有回应。一个真正靠谱的人，必定是一个谦逊的人，在他们的身上，你看不到自大、傲慢不可一世，更看不到夸夸其谈、居功自傲。他们总是为人低调、谦卑踏实，不吹嘘自己的成就，不看低他人的努力，而是认真踏实地、一步一个脚印地耕耘自己的事业。比如池勇海先生，他总是给大家一种稳重踏实、靠谱的感觉，大家都愿意和他搭档，组成团队

As the Chinese saying goes, we must keep good companions as we travel and good neighbors as we reside.

It matters with whom we get together in the world, as companions may affect our lives. As we keep their company, we may become very much like them. By being among excellent people and by growing up bravely, we will stand at an even higher level, see different scenes and make a difference.

I have credible, positive people around me. They are credible in that they handle everything entrusted to them and give firm responses. Truly credible persons are certainly humble ones. They are never arrogant or full of hot air, and they never claim credit for themselves. Instead, they keep a low profile, seemingly humble and steadfast. They are disgusted with bragging about achievements or belittling the efforts of

一起做项目。他遇到困难，表现的是不逃避、敢于担当，遇到问题反省自身、主动承担责任、坦坦荡荡、光明磊落、不掖不藏。他是靠着自己的才能和努力，兢兢业业、脚踏实地工作，收获他人的信任，与他相处久了，必然会受到影响，踏实做事，自己的格局也会越来越大，也会得到他人的重视，人生路会越走越宽。

others. They are serious and steadfast in cultivating their own careers step by step. Dennis, for instance, is such a man, steady and reliable. Everyone wants to partner with him to team up for projects. When in trouble, he will never escape but take his responsibility. When he encounters problems, he will reflect on himself first and take the initiative to assume responsibility in a frank, open way. He shows his abilities and works hard in a conscientious and down-to-earth manner, gaining the trust of others. Having got along with him for some time, we are inevitably influenced to broaden our visions and work in a down-to-earth approach, and we will be taken seriously. This way, our road of life will become even wider.

同时他也是一个充满着正能量的人，内心充满阳光，带有正能量磁场，一直跟大家说做人要儒雅，要有风度。遇到事情，从不抱怨，表现得很沉着冷静，这种情绪常常感染着我们，不仅因为他有正能量，还因为他能让我们也释放出正能量。大家都喜欢和他聊天，无论是从工作说到生活，从朋友说到家庭，还是从过去到现在再到将来，总有意犹未尽的感觉。就算是阴天，他心里也装着太阳，让身边的人常常信心倍增，感受到人性的光辉和社会的美好。大家跟他在一起共事感觉是安心、放松、愉悦的，感受到生命的意义和生活的趣味。因此，我们都喜欢正能量的人，因为他真的自带光芒！

Dennis is also a man of positive energy, cheerful in the heart. He's been telling us to behave with grace. He never complains in face of difficulties but deals with them calmly. His mood inspires us, letting us release positive energy. We enjoy chatting with him on topics from work to life, from friends to family, from the past to the present and to the future, as if there were a lot more things left unsaid. He radiates cheerful sunshine even in cloudy days doubling the confidence of people around him so that they feel the glory of human nature and the beauty of the society. We feel safe, relaxed and pleasant working with him and experience the significance and joy of life. As a result, we all like him, as he is a man of positive energy beaming his own light!

要想持续地释放出正能量，就要和有正能量的人在一起，一边吸收正能量，一边释放正能量，吸放之间，生命恒新。一个人的能量是有限的，不同人的能量场的强度也是不同的，但有相同梦想的人，能量是能够相加的。人生路上处处是险滩，一定要和充满正能量、靠谱的人同行，少走弯路，成就最好的自己。

If we are to incessantly release positive energy, we have to meet people with positive energy and absorb the positive energy while releasing it, keeping life constantly afresh. A person's energy is limited. It varies in intensity among different people, but people cherishing the same dreams may aggregate their energies. Life is full of dangers. We must forge ahead with credible people who are full of positive energy, avoid detours and perfect ourselves.

姜 洁
Tina Jiang

作为一个7岁小女孩的妈妈，在陪伴孩子的过程中发现不只是孩子需要成长，自己也需要不断成长，只有自己变得更好，才有能力把孩子教育得越来越好。慢慢地，你会在孩子成长的过程中，发现TA的身上透漏着你的气质。你的动作，你的话语，甚至是你的脾气都在影响着TA。因为你努力的样子，孩子也看得到。

As the mother of a seven-year-old little girl, Tina Jiang has realized, while being with the child, that not only the child but also herself need to grow constantly. Only when you have become better yourself can you educate your children and help them become better. Gradually, you will find your temperament reflected in your children while they are growing. A child is influenced by your gestures, speeches or even your temper. The way you make efforts is also being watched by your children.

回首 2019
Looking Back on 2019

■ Dorothy Hua

有错过才会有新的遇见，缘分就是，不早不晚，恰恰刚好，正如进入 CNOOD 这个大家庭。现在回想起来，第一次面试时的心情至今仍印象深刻，内心的忐忑、紧张，生怕哪个问题回答得不够完美。在面试结束后，仍会回想当时的每个细节，仔细思量是否有过不妥。幸运的是，在不久之后便收到了回复，当时激动的心情久久不能平复。人生中的第一份工作赋予了它不同的意义，是一个新的起点，新的挑战，也是一个重要的转折点。

曾经经常听到的一句话，今日你以育才为荣，明日育才以你为荣。当时可能只是一笑而过，现在回想起来，不知怎的，有些许感动。不知今日的我是否让你骄傲。做了20多年的学生，突然间的角色

It's only by missing some chances in life that we gain new encounters. Predestination is precisely something that happens just in time, coming neither too early nor too late. The same is true of gaining access to the CNOOD family. Now as I look back, I still have a vivid picture of my first interview. I was ill at ease, for fear that I could not give the perfect answers. As the interview ended, I recalled every detail, wondering whether anything went wrong. Fortunately, I received a response shortly thereafter. I was so excited at that time. The first job in my life certainly had a special meaning, as it was a new start, a new challenge and a key turning point.

At School, I often heard the words: today, you are proud to go to Yucai; tomorrow, Yucai will be proud to have you as an aluminus. I just laughed it off in those days. Now as I recall it, I'm a

转换，在不太适应的同时感受到一份新的责任，是对自己选择的坚持，是对旁人信任的感激，也是一份对社会的回馈。对于财务工作，不再单单是学生期间一些片面的理解，一个个数字，一张张图表，褪去它们枯燥的表述方式，单刀直入地将财务状况剖析得简单明了，直击人心。

初出茅庐的我们，在不经意间叩响社会的大门，跨入门槛的第一步仍是学习，不同于书本上的知识，实践中的学习更为直观深刻。例如，在接触 EPC 项目的过

little touched. I am wondering whether I have made you proud today. Having been a student for more than 20 years, I suddenly had a new role, and I felt a new responsibility as I managed to get adapted. It is to stick to my choice, to be grateful for others' trust, and to give back to the society. Financial work is no longer what I understood it to be in my school years — mere figures and charts. Getting rid of the boring way of expression, they come straight to the point in analyzing financial situations.

Young and inexperienced, we knocked at the door of the society as if by accident. The first step across the threshold still means learning new things. Other than the

程中，学习到前期的预算、执行期间的跟踪及后期的控制的重要性。缅甸项目将海外施工的优缺点都完整地暴露出来，为下一次的EPC项目提供了良好的反面教材。取其精华，弃其糟粕。前一次的经验教训都是为下一次的完美成功做铺垫。在上海培训中，学习到不同的国际贸易术语及相关的法律问题，出口货物的风险管理，合同中易忽视的风险点，海外工作需注意的事项等。这些学习抛开了老师的提问，抛开了考卷的测试，将在真刀真枪的实践中得到检验。

在人生的旅途中，总会遇到形形色色的人，发生各种各样的事，有的留下浓墨重彩的一笔，有的挥一挥手悄然远去，有的至今仍伴左右，有的早已淡出舞台。而2019年，作为人生中短暂的一年，有过迷茫、彷徨，有过拼搏、奋斗，有过心酸、孤独，有过甜蜜、喜悦，感受过酸甜苦辣，才能不畏生活；告别了青春岁月的他们，遇见了风华正茂的你们，经历过风风雨雨，才能直面人生。在接下来的旅途中，不忘初心，携手同行。

knowledge in books, learning in practice becomes more intuitive and profound. For example, when I was engaged in the EPC project, I learned the importance of budgeting in the early stage, tracking in the implementation and controlling in the late stage. The Myanmar project is a showcase of the advantages and disadvantages of overseas construction, providing a negative example for future EPC projects. As the ancients said, we should take the essence and discard the dregs. Lessons from past experiences are the foundation on which to achieve perfect success in the future. In the Shanghai training program, I learned various international trade terms and related legal issues, risk management of export goods, risk points easily overlooked in contracts and issues to note in overseas work. During these studies, there are no teachers' questions and test papers, but we are tested in real business in the world.

In the journey of life, we will encounter all kinds of people and experience all sorts of things. Some of them add thick and deep-colored brushes in our lives, but others we just wave off; some are still around us, while others have faded offstage. The year 2019 was a transient moment in my life. I had confusions and losses, struggles and striving. I felt sad and lonely but also harvested sweetness and joy. Only when we have tasted the joys and sorrows of life will we be dauntless in the journey ahead,

as those bidding farewell to the youthful days meet new friends in their prime. Having lived through the ups and downs, we will confront our lives. In the next journey, let's keep in mind our original aspirations and move forward hand in hand.

华 霞
Dorothy Hua

华霞，浙江人，作为最不像95后的95后，最不像天蝎座的天蝎座，开心做人，踏实做事。

Dorothy Hua, a native of Zhejiang Province, was born after 1995 and was born a scorpio. However, She does not share the traits of the post-1995 generation or a Scorpio. Her creed is to be happy in life and earnest at work.

成长的意义

The Significance of Growth

■ Billy Gu

题目有些大，这并不是我所要总结的，而是我一直在寻求的，也许是正处于当下环境的影响里（全球新冠肺炎疫情的蔓延）才使得自己真正能面对自我，回顾一下这十年来，我生命的沉淀。

This subject seems a little big. It is not something I'm to probe into but a goal I've been seeking all these years. Perhaps it is due to the current environment, the global pandemic of COVID-19, that enables me to truly face up to myself and look back what I have accumulated over the past 10 years.

也再次声明，本文谨代表个人肤浅的体验和个人的生命历程，并不是所谓的"鸡汤"，希望能给予本人一些警醒，能时刻提醒自我在做人、做事上的欠缺。对于家庭的责任的担当，对于我个人信仰的持守，对于工作的态度上，坚持健康的持续的追求。

时间一晃而过，公司的业务发展已过十载，我在CNOOD也已然十年了。历历在目的不止是公司在十年内翻天覆地的变化，更是在十年中对于自我认知的沉淀，对于工作原则的建立，对于各样责任的明确。曾经池总教诲道：年轻人有三个重要的十年。一不小心已入第二个十年，此时正是一个绝好的机会，本文的主旨也正是让自己从不时的虚假自欺中觉醒，警醒明辨自己信仰的持守，对家庭的担当、工作的态度等是非与真伪，望能及时纠正思想和行为上的不义。

我坚信：一个对家人同事朋友有担当，为人处事上有能力的人，必定是一位持着感恩的心、谦卑受教的人。在这点上，我有权时刻提醒自己，因为我深知本我的亏欠，对于处事为人上的骄傲，常常影响自己的生活和工作。我很幸运的是，我确定了我一生的信仰追求。这不但促使自己建立并不断完善对于工作的原则，持续思考工作的意义。了解自己对于家庭、

I'd like to expressly declare this article represents only my superficial personal experience in my life course. It's not a "chicken soup for the soul." I hope it gives me some alert and constantly reminds me the deficiencies in my life and work. It is a showcase of my responsibility for the family, my conviction to the faith, my attitude to work and my persistent pursuit of health.

How time flies. The business has been going on for over 10 years. I've also been in CNOOD for over 10 years. What have come to my mind are not only earth-shaking changes of the company but also accumulated self-knowledge, established work principles and clear-cut responsibilities. Dennis told us that young people should take seriously three crucial 10 years. Before I know it, I have entered the second 10 years. This is a golden opportunity. I write it down exactly for the purpose of alerting myself of false self-deception from time to time and identifying my beliefs, family responsibilities and work attitudes, in the hope of duly correcting ideological and behavioral misconducts.

I firmly believe that a person responsible for his or her family, colleagues and friends and capable of treating others honestly must be a grateful and modest person. In this regard, I should remind myself at all times, as I am aware of my deficiency—my pride in dealing with others and things—which often affects my life and work. I am

同事、朋友的担当是什么。

我不依靠各种所谓的"心灵鸡汤"，这些使人突发的激进（激发进取），并不是长远稳定的。真正的激励在于内在心灵产生实际改变的结果。往往我会颠倒"我的激进是否源于促使我激进的动机"还是"我的激进是明确意义从而真正激励了自己的结果"。过去的十年中，浮现在脑海中的状态，从迷茫地去接受各种任务到学会初步的为人处事；心态的处理从遇事焦躁不安到所谓的"坦然无惧"。需要强调的是，这种过程的转变，有一个核心的

fortunate that I have confirmed the faith of my life. It pushes me to establish and constantly improve the principles of work, to keep thinking about the significance of work, to understand my responsibilities for my family, colleagues and friends.

I don't rely on the "chicken soups for the soul," as these sudden inspirations won't last long. The real motivation brings actual changes in our inner minds. I would often confuse "my aggressiveness motivated by the motives that push me to be radical" with "my aggressiveness as a result of having a clear idea of the significance which really inspires me." Over the past decade, I have advanced from accepting all tasks in confusion to

瓶颈，我在这些年来发现和学会相对控制的时候很滞后，导致对于工作和生活的态度变得极其狭隘，并以此为荣。这就是人性的骄傲，希望分享这个自己的软弱，并希望能提醒到自己，时刻地警醒自己在修炼的路上要攻克己心，避免此内在情绪的泛滥。回顾过去，并不是我学会了为人处事，也并非遇事坦然了，而且是自己在积累中得到的些许的经验以及教训；但这完全不值得任何的推崇和学习，仅仅作为一种今后路程中的借鉴。时刻倒空自己，才能被充满，若是执念于之前的所获所得，就必无法得到新的启发和收获。

我很庆幸在这十年中，有诸多贵人给我指点、拍打、教诲，并如此宽容、忍耐那稚嫩又叛逆的我。我们的岁月静好，常常是因为我们前辈和长辈的负重前行。我们或许不都了解公司的发展历程是如何艰辛，或许我们不都明白自己在公司的意义是什么，但有一点我能坚定认同的是，没有任何事情是容易且不需要付出代价的。在现在这样特殊的艰难的环境中，我们唯

learning the art of dealing with all kinds of people and things. In this process, I have progressed from feeling restless when anything crops up to "meeting them calmly and undauntedly." It's important to note that there's a core bottleneck in this shift. Over the years I have found and learned that there is a lag in relative control which leads to an extremely narrow attitude towards work and life that I was once proud of. This is the pride in human nature. I share this weakness of mine in the hope that I could constantly alert myself to conquer it on the road of self-cultivation and avoid the spread of this inner emotion. Looking back on the past, I have not yet learned how to deal with others and things, and I have not yet been fully at ease when misgivings crop up, but I have gained some experience and lessons in the process of accumulation. It is unworthy of praise or imitation, just a reference in the way forward. We have to empty ourselves before we are to be filled. If we are obsessed with what we have gained in the past, we will be unable to get new inspirations and harvests.

I feel lucky that in the past decade, I have met a lot of people who are ready to give me advice and urge me to forge ahead. They are so tolerant to me who was young and rebellious. We are enjoying a quiet life because our elders have taken the heavy loads for us. We may not know how hard the company has been in the process of expansion.

独能做的就是做好自己。但是问题来了：到底何为"做好自己"？我入公司的第一天，池总就教诲我们要做好自己，至今也只能略懂一二。一个能"做好自己"的人，个人认为是有坚定且明确的目标，在生活和工作上极度自律的人。这是我们一生的功课，我承认在这点上，我自己是做得极其不够的，时常患得患失，目标的模糊、个人的懒散，这是普遍的现象。我发现时间的流逝真等不起我如此的挥霍，无论是在信仰的持守，还是工作生活的状态上。"我也知道在我里头，就是我肉体之

We may have no idea what our roles are in the company. However, I agree with one thing — nothing is easy and costless. In such an especially hard time, the only thing we can do is to be ourselves. Then, there comes the question — how to be ourselves? The first day I joined the company, Dennis told us to be ourselves. Now I know a little bit of it. A person who can "be himself/herself" must have a firm and clear goal and be self-disciplined in life and work. This is the lesson in

中，没有良善。因为立志为善由得我，只是行出来由不得我。"（《圣经·新约·罗马书》）但这并不是作为放弃自我的理由，同样，我在这边再次重提，明确这些我自己的问题，并不是要让别人认同，而是为了时刻警醒自己，别忘记自己需要时常感恩前辈的付出、同事的努力，家人的无私、朋友的帮助，他们并非欠我什么，而这些是否是我应得的呢？答案往往不是。

我想就先谈到这里，我们的路很长，同时我们的时间却是十分的短暂，一不留神那本需要我们努力的时刻就会逝去，一不小心就迷失了自我与浮世沉沦，哪里还有时间自我思考，自我学习，自我警醒。自由而无用的灵魂，谦卑地修炼自己，对于那些不想做的事情可以不做，感恩地去面对出现在我生命中的所有人，或许是在患难中使我们学会忍耐，从忍耐中学会老练，老练中生出盼望。

加油，写给2020年的自己，也写给2030年回顾我在CNOOD第二个十年的那时候的自己。

our lives. I admit I have not done good enough in this regard. I am often swayed by consideration of gaines and losses, have unclear targets and become indolent. This is a universal phenomenon. I have found that time goes by so fast. I shall not idle away, no matter in belief or in work and life. It has been stipulated in the book of Romans in the Bible, "For I know that in me (that is, in my flesh) dwelleth no good thing; for to will is present with me; but how to perform that which is good, I find not." That is not an excuse for giving up ourselves. Similarly, I have to stress again that I am identifying my problems not to win others' approval but to remind myself that I should be grateful for the dedications of the seniors, the efforts of the colleagues, the care of the family and the assistance of my friends. They don't owe me anything. Do I deserve all these? The answer is often negative.

I'll stop here. We have a long way to go, and yet our time is so short. If we are not careful enough, we may lose the moments when we should work hard, get lost and sink into depravity. Then we will not have the time to think for ourselves, learn for ourselves and be alert for ourselves. As free and useless souls, we may humbly cultivate ourselves, avoid the things we don't want to do and be thankful for all the people in our lives.

Let's go for it. These lines are for myself in 2020 and for myself in 2030 when I will look back on my second 10 years in CNOOD.

顾天阳
Billy Gu

2010年正式加入CNOOD工作至今，现为高级客户经理，MBA学历。见证了CNOOD每一次起点，每一次奇迹的发生。从一般贸易到工程贸易，从工程贸易到项目采购中心，现在又在为公司成为真正的EPC工程公司而努力。相信：一切不是最好就没到最后。

Billy has been working at CNOOD since he formally joined the company in 2010 with an MBA degree. Now, he is a senior account manager at CNOOD. He has witnessed every starting point of CNOOD and every time a miracle has occurred. Having witnessed the transformation of CNOOD from a company focused on general trade to one engaged in engineering trade, and again to a project procurement center, now he is making efforts to help CNOOD become a true EPC company. He believes that it is not the end if everything is not the best.

光从哪里来

The Source of Light

■ Jane Yan

从2013年底我作为一名毕业生加入施璐德，到现在成长为一名项目经理，6年的时间，我认识了很多人，也让很多人认识了我。这不长但也不短的6年里，我的人生产生了很多不一样的可能性，个人生活状态的变化、辗转，一切的思索、感受与困惑，一帧一帧，都在其间。

光阴荏苒

我即将分享的这些感受，我把它取名叫：光从哪里来。

我

入职的第四年可谓职业生涯的至暗时刻，工作上遇到一些瓶颈难以突破，所以那个时候，我特别郁闷。每天早上一睁开眼，想到要去公司上班，完全没有动力。我也觉得我每天都在做重复性劳动，感觉

In late 2013, I joined CNOOD after leaving the campus. In the past six years, I have grown from a green hand to a project manager. In this period, I have met all sorts of people and displayed myself to them. The six years are not long but not short either. They have brought about changes in my life, recording all my thoughts, feelings and confusions, like a camera, frame by frame.

Time flies!

The following are some of my perceptions I'm about to share, titled "The Source of Light".

Me

The fourth year after I took the job proved the darkest in my career. I met some bottlenecks at work which I was unable to break. I was depressed. Every morning after I opened eyes, I was vexed

很焦虑，又不知道该怎么办。

我追问着自己：现在的状态是不是我想要的？是继续待在重复的舒适区，还是走出来寻找更多的可能性？我不断地思考这个问题，然后反思了很多从工作第一年到第四年的种种经历，我的内心发出了一束光：我要找一个出口，重新认识自己，我一定要改变。

翻阅名人大牛的书，接触一些优秀人士的经历，我慢慢了解到，令"我之所以是我"的，是我身上那些最有价值的特质，比如说独立、自尊自爱、坚持自己的声音、关心社会与他人等，而不是因为别人寄托在我身上的点评或标签，亦不是我自身的想象。这种认知，让我开始变得自信。

to think I should go to the company, so I was out of steam. I was doing repetitive work every day, and I was at a loss what to do next.

I asked myself, "Is this what I want?" Shall I stay to enjoy the comfort of repetitive work or go out to look for more possibilities? I was obsessed with the question, while reflecting on my work experience over the past four years. Then a beam of light emitted from my heart, telling me I should find an outlet and rediscover myself. I should make a change.

I leafed through many books of celebrities to learn about their experiences. I realized that what made me were precisely the most valuable traits in me, i.e., independence, self-respect, standing up to myself and caring about the society and others. They were not labels placed on me by others, nor my own imagination. With this knowledge, I became more confident.

我开始希望在世界中扮演一个主动的角色，无论是学习、工作、婚姻、生育、积累财富等任何一种。我希望自己成为这样一种人：拥有善良、正义、担当，不管在多么困难的境地下，在多么黑暗的夜里，都不会失去希望和内心的光明，并且能够用最好的生命状态去感染更多人。

种一棵树，最好的时间是十年前，其次是现在。

我这样想时，那常挂在嘴角的微笑和行走时带起的风，它们都告诉我，世界开始不一样。

在这个慌乱而匆忙的时代，还有比这更柔软、更坚定的勇敢吗？

你说光从哪里来？去做更好的自己，内心的光就一定会驱散阴霾，指明方向。

工作

我相信每个人上学的时候，都会有一种经历——害怕别人说自己努力。那时候总觉得，如果需要努力才能做成一件事，可真丢人啊！所以会跟其他同学说：我放学回家基本不学习。

实际上呢？你每天晚上，做题到凌晨一点钟……

现在想想，努力有什么丢人的呢？不努力才丢人！

持续努力的学习，就是让一个人成为Plus+的自己。主动学习，才能适应时代。成功的人，都是时间的长期主义者，把学

I started to hope to play an active role in this world, in the fields of study, work, marriage, fertility and wealth. I wanted to be such a person, who, equipped with kindness, justice and responsibility, would never lose hope and inner light no matter how difficult the situation and how dark the night might be. Instead, in the best state of life, I would inspire more people.

The best time to plant a tree should be 10 years ago. But it's not too late now.

As I thought so, the smiles at the corners of my mouth and the light steps I took told me that the world started to be different.

In this frantic, hurried age, is there any softer, firmer courage?

So where is the source of light? Be a better self, and the light in our hearts will dispel the haze and point the way.

Work

I am sure everyone has such an experience in the school days—we fear others say that we work hard. I felt that it was a shame to make efforts to get something done, so I often told my classmates I barely studied after going home.

But in fact, every night I did homework until round midnight.

Now as I look back, I realize that it doesn't make a scene to study hard. It's embarrassing on the contrary.

Keeping to study hard is to make us surpass ourselves. By taking the initiatve to study, we will adapt to the times.

习的目标植根于长期的坚持不懈,不盲从几天的变化,也不低估几个月几年的变化,终会长出丰硕的果实。

是的,要学习。那么,学什么?

互联网时代,大规模碎片化的知识最容易习得,但如果不能结合思维能力去解决具体问题,市场价值几乎等于零。

我们常常忘了,人的大脑,不应该只用来记忆,更重要的是用来思考。

《奇葩说》里陈铭举过一个例子:水在零度的时候会结冰,这是一个常识,是对外部客观规律的归纳和总结。而在未来的时间中,我在什么时候把什么味道的水变成什么味道的冰棒,再卖给谁,这就叫作对知识的智慧运用和处理能力。

High-flyers are all long-termists. They root the goal of learning in long-term perseverance. They neither blindly follow changes in a few days nor underestimate changes in a few months and years. Fruitful results will grow in the end.

It's true that we must learn. Then, what shall we learn?

In the Internet age, it's easy to acquire massive fragmented knowledge. However, if we cannot solve specific problems with the ability of thinking, these efforts are close to zero in market value.

It often slips our mind that human brain should not be used only for memory. They shall be applied to think.

Chen Ming cited a case in the variety show *Qi Pa Shuo*: Water freezes at zero. It is a common sense, the induction and summary of an external objective law. But when shall I turn water of some tastes into popsicles and sell them? This is

从这个层面上讲，这种学习后产生的"独立思考和解决问题"的能力，正是值得投入更多的精力的、不局限于行业和岗位的、更高级的、可迁移的能力。对于职业发展来说，通过修习这样的能力来不断完善自己、打开自己，而后再反馈给事业，和它一起成长，是一种非常理想的状态。

the ability to use and handle knowledge intelligently.

In this case, the ability to "think and solve problems independently" after learning is a more advanced and transferable ability that deserves extra efforts, and it is not limited to one industry or position. For career development, it is ideal to constantly improve ourselves, unfold ourselves by practicing this ability, feed it back to our career and grow up

世上工作千万种，往往最为难得是"适合你"。适合是催化剂，可以将一个人的天赋与才能发挥到极致。当某项工作还未开始，你已经迫不及待地跃跃欲试，并且非常有信心能做好，你做这项工作得到的必将比别人多，成长、进步得比别人快，甚至于即使做到疲劳和困倦，也往往感觉异常满足，因为你找到了足够匹配自己兴趣的职业方向。

可是我们当中的大多数，往往没有那么幸运，完全匹配的工作常常可遇不可求。日趋激烈的行业竞争，企业的发展和淘汰几乎是一夕之间。现代企业，要提高效率，降低风险，必然走向专业化分工，然而专业化分工的同时也在专业化地"选人"，并不依赖个人的"情感适合"，这对人才来说是灾难性的。

在这种趋势下，应该如何处理个人与职业的关系呢？

这个时候需要思考：
这个行业和公司的关键成功因素是什么？对用户对社会的价值是什么？我的岗位对公司的核心价值是什么？

这几个问题的答案，都可以用一句话概括：解决问题。

There are numerous jobs in the world. The rarest is the one that "fits us." Fitting is a catalyst, as it takes our talent and ability to the fullest. If we can't wait to get into work before it starts and have the confidence to do it well, we will gain more from this job and grow faster than others. Even if we are fatigued and drowsy in this process, we will feel unusually content since we have found the career direction that matches our interest.

However, most of us are often not so lucky. Perfectly matched jobs are hard to come by. In the increasingly fierce industry competition, the development or elimination of a business often takes place overnight. A modern enterprise will inevitably choose specialized division of labor to improve efficiency and reduce risks. However, specialized division of labor also implies professionalized "selection of talent," which does not depend on personal "emotional fitness." This is disastrous for talents.

In this circumstance, how shall we deal with the relationship between an individual and the career?

We must think:

What are the key factors to make an industry or a business a success? What are the values to the users and the society? What is the core value of my post to the company?

The answers to these questions can be summed up in one phrase—solving problems.

任何职业，本质都是学习并解决问题。营销解决的是如何让客户知道我们的产品和服务，HR 解决的是如何让公司有充足的人才供给等。公司也是某类用户或社会问题的一套抽象而具体的解决方案，比如滴滴解决快速打车需求，饿了么解决居家用餐需求。

能解决问题，个人或者公司就有了存在的价值。

所以学习的最终目的是为了解决问题，这很重要。

从更加宏观的角度去看问题，而不是去做一颗螺丝钉；使自己横向可迁移、纵向可拓展，而不是被定制；把自己的发展和公司的命运紧密相连，共同面对并解决发展的难题。

不同阶段炼化不同的素质，丰富、拓展自己解决问题的能力与方式，就可以"以不变应万变"，从而"干一行、爱一行"，完成个人与职业双向关系的良好传递与反馈。

经历告诉我，无论是对未来迷茫也好，遇到发展瓶颈也好，其实都可以去解决的。我们要做的，就是去学习，将学到的知识内化成独立思考的能力、解决问题

Any profession, in essence, is to learn and solve problems. Marketing addresses the problem of how to let customers know about the products and services. HR solves the problem of how to supply the company with enough talent. A company is an abstract or concrete solution for certain types of users or social problems. For instance, DiDi meets the need for fast ride-hailing. Eleme delivers take-out to the door.

An individual or a company has the value of existence once they can solve problems.

So the ultimate goal of learning is to solve problems. It's important to remember this.

We must see the issues from a macro perspective rather than serving as a cog We must expand ourselves extensively rather than being customized. We must closely link our own development with the fate of the company and together face and solve development problems.

At different stages, we must cultivate different qualities, enrich and expand our competence and develop ways to solve problems so as to "cope with shifting events by sticking to a fundamental principle" and "love whatever job we take up." Thus, we can complete the sound transmission and feedback between one's personal life and professional life.

My experience tells me that whether we are confused about the future or meet development bottlenecks, we can actually solve them. What we should do

的能力，就能形成独特的个人品牌，更裨益于个人与工作的共同发展。

你说光从哪里来？饱满的求知欲和源源不断的自我驱动实践能力，可以照亮事业发展的时空大道。

小世界

在施璐德的这几年里，我结婚、生子，如今儿子两岁多了。

两岁的小孩，就像一个电量永远满格的发电机，爱跳、爱跑、爱探索一切新鲜事物。

这个小小的生命，能在不经意间戳破我自以为是伪装成"大人"的壳，时刻提醒我：宝宝只是年纪小，不要欺负宝宝读书少。

is to learn and internalize our knowledge into an ability to think independently and solve problems. This way, we will establish a unique personal brand, which is conducive to the common development of the individual and the work.

So what is the source of light? Our thirst for knowledge and incessant self-driven abilities to put ideas into practice may illuminate the space-time avenue for career development.

A Little World

During my years at CNOOD, I got married and had a son, who is over two years old now.

A 2-year-old boy is like a fully-charged generator, loving to jump, run and explore everything new.

This little life will poke by accident through the "adult" shell which I self-righteously put on, reminding me all the time that a little baby may have great

经常是前一秒被他怼到满头黑线，下一秒却觉得娃说得甚有道理。那些或扎心或暖心的时刻，不光让我觉得智商被碾压，更让我窥见一个纯真又缤纷的小宇宙，它藏在一个稚气童真的小脑袋瓜里，不定期向成年人开放。

某一天再回过头来想起，你会发现那些自然天成的小哲理，还有让人捧腹的小俏皮，像宝石一样闪闪发亮，成为我最宝贵的记忆。

而作为父母的我，能给孩子最好的礼物，就是足够的爱和包容。

让他的眼里永远有星星，心里永远有诗……

你说光从哪里来？小孩子的童真，就可以点亮一个充满爱和幸福的小世界。

尾

2019年，是施璐德成立十周年。

十年，除了对旧时光的感慨，最重要的是在我们身处的每一个坐标系中，留下了我们奋斗、思考和经历的共同印记。

时间沉淀记忆，记忆引领未来。我相信，过去的十年发生的一切，都将引导我们走向一条更正确的、更长远的道路。

就像十年之前，即使我们互不认识，但相似的灵魂总会相遇。

He often dissed me and made me speechless, but in a second I would find that he made sense. Those heart-piercing and heart-warming moments made me feel overwhelmed and allowed me to peek at a pure and colorful microcosm that is hidden in the childish little head, open occasionally to adults.

One day as I look back, I will find that the natural philosophic thoughts and the hilarious witty remarks of the little child will still shine like gems and become my most precious memories.

As a mom, the best gift I can give him is enough love and tolerance.

Let there always be stars in his eyes and poetry in his heart.

So what is source of light? Children's innocence can light up a little world of love and happiness.

Epilogue

The year 2019 marked the 10th anniversary of the founding of CNOOD.

In addition to deep feelings about the old time, the 10 years, most important of all, have left a common mark of our struggles, thoughts and experiences in every coordinate system we are in.

Time precipitates memory, and memory leads to the future. I believe what has happened over the past decade will lead us to a more correct and long-lasting path.

It's just like 10 years ago—even if we didn't know each other, similar souls

如今，这么多志同道合的伙伴聚在一起，如同微光会吸引微光，微光会照亮微光，然后一起发光，穿透雾霾，把前路照亮。

would always meet.

Today, so many like-minded friends have rallied here, like glimmer attracts twilight, illuminating each other. They will shine together to penetrate the haze and light the way ahead.

闫京亚
Jane Yan

毕业于上海大学机械工程专业，2014年7月加入施璐德。感性工科女，靠谱金牛座。认真工作，热爱生活。愿用无比真诚和不断向上的初心与这个特别的集体共振。

Jane graduated from Shanghai University majoring in mechanical engineering and joined CNOOD in July 2014. She is a sentimental female engineer and a dependable Taurus. She works hard and loves life. She wishes to resonate with this unique organization with her usual sincerity and original aspiration of making continuous progress.

一缕思绪

A Wisp of Thought

■ Jeff Xu

朋友跟我说，他最近睡眠质量很差，难以入睡，睡着了又整晚整晚地做梦，疲惫不堪。

这时我会告诉朋友，近三年我一躺床上就能睡着，一觉就能睡到天大亮，而且不带做梦的，你敢信？

朋友觉得不可思议，非常羡慕我能有这么好的睡眠。于他而言，能睡个没有梦的安稳觉，是非常奢侈的。当时的我还挺庆幸，与朋友相比，不受失眠多梦折磨的我的确挺值得这份羡慕。但仔细一想却挺可悲的，什么时候开始，自己连做梦的能力都没有了。

古人语：人生百岁，七十稀少，更除十年孩童小。又十年昏老，都五十载，一

A friend of mine recently complained to me that he had trouble falling asleep. He said that even if he fell asleep, he would dream all night long, which made him fatigued to the extreme.

I told him that in the past three years, I can fall asleep the moment I get into bed. I can sleep until dawn without dreaming. "Do you believe it？" I asked him.

My friend felt incredible. He envied me for having such a sound sleep. It was a luxury for him to have a dreamless sleep. At that time I felt quite lucky. Compared with him, I deserved the envy for not suffering from insomnia and excessive dreams, but on second thought, I found it quite sad. I don't know since when I have lost the ability to dream.

As an ancient Chinese saying goes, a man seldom lives to be seventy years old.

半被睡魔分了。那二十五载之中，宁无些个烦恼。这句话本意是人生短暂，倡导人们珍惜时光，把握当下，过好生命中的每一天。

In the first 10 years, we are too young. In the last 10 years, we are too old. Of the 50 years in the prime of life, we spend a half in dreams. According to this caculation, we live only for 25 years, and we would rather not to have any worry during this short time. The saying, in its original meaning, is to stress that life is short and to remind us that we should cherish the time, seize the day and live a good life every day.

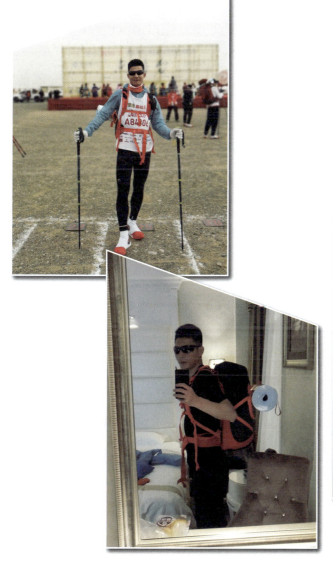

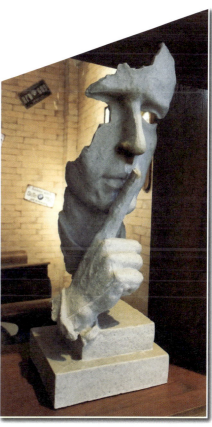

从内容上来说，个人觉得未免有些消极。十年少小，是每个人一生中最纯真最快乐的阶段；而十年昏老，孔子不也说过六十而耳顺，七十而从心所欲；至于一半又在梦中，谁又敢说，醒着的整日忙碌奔波，就一定比睡着的梦境更有价值？

德国哲学家黑格尔曾说：存在即合理。我觉得挺有道理的。

梦存在于每个人的生活中，必定有它的意义。然而梦的存在太过普通，就像空气，我们很少去思考它的价值和意义。只有当没有了空气，人才会意识到空气的重要性。我想，梦也是如此。

睡着的时候，梦中的世界，天马行空，往往比醒着的现实世界丰富精彩得多。J.K.罗琳在咖啡馆写出了魔幻小说《哈利·波特》系列，我一直很好奇，她是怎么想出来的。我坐在咖啡馆，脑子里怎么只有店员、咖啡以及形形色色的客人。后来，我突然觉得，哈利·波特很有可能就活在J.K.罗琳的梦里，她只是醒来之后找了个咖啡馆，及时把梦境记录了下来并加以后期创作。

我相信，许多科幻电影里的场景，不是艺术家坐在咖啡馆里凭空想出来了，而是梦，很有可能就是艺术家们灵感源泉，

In terms of the contents, I feel it is a little negative. The first 10 years are the purest, happiest period in our lives. In the last 10 years, as Confucius put it, we can understand whatever we hear without exertion and follow whatever our hearts desire without transgressing the law. As for spending half of the 50 prime years in dreams, who could say that our awakened days, with us busily rushing about all day long, are more valuable than dreams?

German philosopher Georg Wilhelm Friedrich Hegel once said that all existence has its reason. I think it makes sense.

Dreams exist in everyone's life, and it must mean something. However, dreams are so common, like air, that we seldom think about its value and significance. Only in the absence of air will we realize the importance of it. I think it is also true with dreams.

The dream world in our sleep is unconstrained, much richer than the waking reality. J.K. Rowling wrote the fantasy novels *Harry Potter* in a cafe. I've been wondering how she came up with it. When I sit in a cafe, why is it all about the waitresses, coffee and guests? Then it occurred to me that Harry Potter might have been living in the dreams of J.K. Rowling. She just woke up to find a cafe to record her dreams in time and created the novels on the basis later.

I believe many scenes of sci-fi movies are not pure imaginations of the artists sitting in cafes. Dreams are most likely a

为电影创作提供了最原始的素材。

我们绝大多数人，晚上睡觉做梦，第二天刚醒来时尚能记得个七七八八。但过不了多久，梦里的内容就会烟消云散。相信大家都有跟身边的人分享自己梦境的经历，但鲜有人会把梦境记录下来。这似乎在某种程度上说明，大部分人，对梦的意义，并没有进行过思考。

我想，梦想的命运，跟梦也大抵差不多，有多少人还能记得自己曾经的梦想？

我记得小时候的梦境丰富多彩、天马行空，为什么长大了，却没有梦了呢？

小孩子的世界，充满了幻想和对未来的美好憧憬，内心所想，无拘无束，就像孙悟空一个筋斗，可以十万八千里，颇有庄子逍遥游的境界。

随着慢慢长大，很多人会越来越认识到自己能力有限，慢慢无意识地给自己设定越来越多的限制，内心所想慢慢也变成了明天的报告怎么写，周五的汇报PPT如何做，诸如此类。更甚者，迷失在工作中，疲惫不堪，脑子里面除了忙碌就是休息。自然而然，睡觉的时候，也就啥都不想了，给自己的大脑按下了关机键，久而

source of inspiration for artists, providing most original materials for film creation.

Most of us sleep and dream at night. When we wake up the next day, we could remember most of the dreams, but it won't be long before the contents of the dreams vanish into thin air. I believe we all have the experience of sharing our dreams with people around us, but few would record the dream scenes. This seems to suggest that to some extent, most people have not seriously thought about the meaning of dreams.

I think the fate of our aspirations might be similar to dreams. How many people still remember their aspirations?

When I was a child, my dreamland was rich and colorful, where I, like a heavenly steed, soared across the skies. Why have I lost my dreams as I grow up?

Children's world is full of fantasy and bright visions for the future. They are unconstrained in minds, like the somersault of the Monkey King Sun Wukong which can reach a distance of over 50,000 km in an instant. It is quite like the realm described by ancient philosopher Chuang-tzu in his *Happy Excursion*.

As we grow up, many people have recognized that they are limited in ability and slowly, unconsciously set more limits on themselves. Their minds have gradually been confined, caring only about how to complete work reports tomorrow or how to make PPT reports on Friday. In some cases, they are simply

久之也就失去了做梦的能力。

当今社会高速发展，人们的生活工作节奏越来越快，我们整日忙碌于工作与社交，在茂密的社会森林中急速穿梭，唯恐慢别人半拍，可又有多少人真正明白自己的终点在哪里。如果每个人的终点不一样，怎么知道谁先到达，又怎么去比较快与慢呢？这个时候，梦就显得尤为重要且珍贵，因为梦的翅膀，能带你飞出这片社会的森林，找到那颗儿时仰望的启明星。

很多人在工作中感受到压力时，往往会变得焦虑暴躁，明明知道焦虑和暴躁不能解决任何问题，反而会对外界以及自身造成一定程度的伤害。但大多数人，却无法停下来，这可能就是别人说的被事情所奴役吧。美国知名冥想导师莎朗·莎兹伯格写过一本《一平方米的静心》，书中分享了一些方法，希望能帮助人们在充满浮躁和焦虑的社会，给自己留出一平方米的空间，心怀梦想，保持正念，从 Doing 的状态中跳出来，进入 Being 的状态。Doing 的状态，是我们和做事之间是分离的，我们被事情所奴役；而 Being 状态，是我们和做事之间是合一的，我们对待事情可以做到收放自如，恬然于心。

lost in work, exhausted to death. Their minds are all about busy work and rest. Naturally, when they fall asleep, they won't think about anything. They've pressed the shutdown button for the brain. Over time, they have lost the ability to dream.

The world is developing at a high speed. Our pace of life and work is getting faster and faster. We are busy with work and socializing all day, shuttling in the dense social forest lest we are half a beat slower than others. How many people really know their destinations? If everyone has a different destination, how do we know who has arrived first, and how do we judge who goes faster? At this time, a dream is particularly important and precious because dreams, spreading their wings, take us to fly out of the social forest and find the Venus we look at in the sky in our childhood.

Many people turn anxious and irritable when they feel the stress at work, although they know that anxiety and irritability cannot solve any problem but only cause harm to others and themselves. However, most people simply cannot stop. This might be that, as some put it, we are enslaved by things. Sharon Salzberg, a famous meditation tutor in the United States, shared some methods in her work *Meditation in One Square Meter* to help people in the restless, anxious society. She proposed to give ourselves a space of one square meter, harbor a dream, maintain mindfulness,

一缕思绪，希望能自我勉励，以梦为马，不负韶华，做最好的自己。加油！

jump out of the state of doing and enter the state of being. In the state of doing, we are separated from things and enslaved by things. In the state of being, we are integrated with things and do things with ease.

I hope to encourage myself with this wisp of thoughts. Let's ride the horse of dreams, live it to the full and be the best of ourselves. Yes, we can do this!

徐志锋
Jeff Xu

2016 年 3 月毕业于上海大学，通过校园招聘与施璐德结缘并有幸成为施璐德大家庭的一分子。

在施璐德的这些年，跟随自己的内心，从心出发，快乐学习，快乐成长，勇敢面对生活和工作中的种种挑战，勇往直前，努力做最好的自己！

Having graduated from Shanghai University in March 2016, Jeff Xu became a member of the big family of CNOOD via campus recruitment. Following and starting from his heart, he has been learning and growing happily during these years at CNOOD. Facing the challenges of both life and work, he is doing his best and marching forward courageously!

感恩相遇　不负遇见
Thank Goodness I Have Met You

■ Heather Zhang

2020年的春天，好似来得特别快，转眼4月就要到了。4月是我的毕业季，意味着我已步入参加工作以来的第七个年头了，但我还依然清晰记得2013年的秋天Dennis和Fay在我们学校校招的场景，记得自己在实习报到那天走进环球世界大厦10楼时的忐忑和兴奋。

如今我们的办公室早已搬至越商大厦，我也从初出茅庐的"新人助理"成长成为一名项目经理，有幸参与并见证了公司的快速发展和转型。Dennis常说未来在年轻人的手中，只有年轻人发展得好，才会有公司的未来。每一年的校园招聘，我都感慨公司招人的门槛越来越高，对专业背景越来越细化，公司的人才结构和储备在不断地升级。

The spring of 2020 seemed to be fleeting. In a wink, April is coming. I graduated in April, which means I've been working for seven years. I still remember the scene in the fall of 2013 when Dennis and Fay came to recruit graduates on our campus. I can also recall the day when I, nervous and exalted, stepped onto the 10th floor of Universal Mansion to start my internship.

Now we have moved our office to Yueshang plaza for a long time. I have also developed from a fledgling "newbie" to witnessing the rapid growth and transformation of the company over the years. Dennis often says that the future lies in the hands of young people. Only when young people have developed well will there be a future for the company. Every year when we recruit staff in the campus, I would feel with emotion that we are raising the threshold

感谢机缘，走出校园的第一份工作就在施璐德。在这里，有专业权威的行业专家，引领年轻人开拓创新；有德高望重的职业导师，成就年轻人的成长；有志同道合的伙伴，互相尊重、信任、透明；有家一样的企业文化，互相关心、创造开心。在这里，每一位同事身上都自带光芒，自信又谦卑。在这里，我经常有一种感觉：如果我不努力，一不留神就会掉队。我想，正是这样"春风细雨、润物无声"的学习氛围塑造了每一位施璐德人。

increasingly higher. We are making detailed requirements on the professional background of the applicants. This way, the company has been upgraded in its talent structure and reserves.

I am grateful to fate that I am lucky enough to have my first job at CNOOD after leaving the campus. Here, we have professional, authoritative industry experts who lead young people to blaze new trails in a pioneering spirit. Here, we have professional mentors of high virtue and glorious name who power the growth of young people. Here, we have like-minded partners who show respect, trust and transparency. And here, we have a family-like corporate culture where we care for each other to create happiness. Everyone brings their own light, confident and yet humble. I often feel that I might fall behind if I do not work hard enough. I think it is exactly such a learning atmosphere, like spring breeze and drizzle, that moisturizes things in silence and shapes every person in CNOOD.

感谢时光，让我遇到了可爱的施璐德家人们。"施璐德的人都跟打了鸡血一样，工作太拼了！""这是施璐德的做事风格。"每次听到这样的评价，我都觉得挺骄傲的，我们在这个行业内起到了旗帜一样的榜样作用。在工作中，我们遇到过非常不信任中国制造的业主监理，也遇到过施工制造环境恶劣并且交货期紧急的项目。因为施璐德的质量控制体系，业主监理从一开始的不信任到项目结束后把我们推荐给其他的业主；因为项目管理优势，我们把不可能赶上的交货期变成了如期交付；因为共同利益，我们牺牲项目成本也要把客户的利益放在第一位；因为团队的力量，我们总是能"化险为夷"，完成一个个看似不可能完成的目标。那些每天两点一线的驻厂时光、在办公室讨论到凌晨的会议、陪业主代表现场检验……这些点点滴滴，回想起来已完全不记得当时的困难和劳累，只记得项目在经过团队努力后得到推动和进展的喜悦和成就感。

感谢施璐德平台，个人的成长离不开公司的培养和投入。从我来到公司，公司

I am grateful to time that I have met the lovely CNOOD family. "The CNOOD people are hyped up at work!" "This is the corporate work style." Every time I hear such comments, I feel proud, as we have now developed into a pacesetter in the industry. In our work, we have met project supervisors on behalf of the proprietors who distrust Chineses manufactures. We have also met projects with poor construction environment and pressing delivery time. Because of our quality control system, the supervisors' attitudes transformed from distrust at the very beginning to offering to recommend us to other business owners at the end of the projects. Because of our competitive project management, we turned an impossible delivery to due delivery. Because of common benefits, we put the customer's interests first despite high project costs. Because of the power of the team, we can always "head off the danger" to accomplish seemingly impossible goals. The time spent to shuttle between the factory and home every day, the meetings held in the office till early morning, the travels accompanying owners' representatives to make on-site inspections …As I recall all these bits and pieces, I have forgotten the difficulties and tiredness. I only remember the joy and accomplishment after our projects were promoted and advanced under the joint efforts of the team.

I am grateful to CNOOD for providing a platform, as our growth is inseparable

组织过性格测试、情绪管理类培训、礼仪培训、职场演讲技能等培训，这些培训让我更了解自己，更懂得要勇敢表达自己，表达欣赏，表达感谢；在专业技能方面，组织不同领域的前辈们给全员做专业采购和项目管理案例分享、IPMP 培训、标准解读学习、FIDIC 合同条款解读等。公司给每一个人最大的权限和信任，每一位新人都有同等的机会独立执行一个项目。另外，在施璐德没有什么比榜样的力量更有影响力了。耳濡目染 Dennis、Fay、Max、Tiger、Tina、石头姐以及其他同事的做人做事的原则，学习他们怎么发展客户，怎么做项目管理，怎么带团队。不管是工作上还是生活中，他们就像大家长一样，关心、帮助每一位后进来的同事。

from the training and investment provided by the company. Soon after I was admitted to the company, I went through personality test, emotional management training, etiquette training and workplace speaking skills training. They let me know more about myself and encouraged me to express myself bravely and speak out appreciation and gratitude. In terms of professional skills, the company has invited senior staff from various fields to share professional procurement and project management cases, conduct IPMP training, conduct standard interpretation and learning and share their interpretation of FIDIC contract terms. It gives everyone the maximum authority and trust, and

感谢自己，每一步都走得坚定和脚踏实地。刚来施璐德的时候，听到最多的灵魂拷问就是：你的兴趣在这里吗？说没有迷茫过是假的，特别是公司这几年业务领域一直在不断地拓宽，每一年都有更优秀的人加入。Dennis 也经常跟我们分享他在公司未来发展的方向和战略上的思考。有的时候我也会怀疑自己：这不是我的专业，我真的能胜任吗？但是我内心又很明确我喜欢这里，我喜欢跟人打交道，我相信自己的学习和适应能力。我告诉自己没有什么害怕的，遇到困难有团队有公司支持我。当有困难和困惑的时候一定要说出来，交流不一定能立刻解决问题，但看问题的不同角度会给我带来新的思路，省去了钻牛角尖甚至绕弯路的风险。事实证

every newcomer has an equal chance to carry out a project independently. There is nothing more influential at CNOOD than the power of role models. I have been influenced by Dennis, Fay, Max, Tiger, Tina Jiang and Tina Xu for their principles of behavior. I have learned from them how to develop clients, manage projects and lead teams. Whether at work or in life, they are like parents, caring and helping every newcomer.

I am grateful to myself for taking each step firmly and down-to-earth. When I first came to CNOOD, the most frequently heard soul-searching question was "Is your interest here?" It would be a lie to say that I have never been lost. These years, the company has been expanding its business fields. Every year, more excellent people join in. Dennis has often shared with us his thinking on the future direction and the strategy of the company. Sometimes I would doubt myself. This is not my major. Can I really do it? However, I am clear in my heart that I like here, that I like to deal with people and that I believe in my ability

明：再长的路，一步步也能走完；再短的路，不迈开双脚也无法到达。只要坚持自己，坚定信念，一定会有好的结果。

"给施璐德十年，还一个全新的自己！"2020年是施璐德下一个十年的开启之年，过去六年，于我自己是一个经验积累和成长蜕变的过程。下一个六年，希望自己能在工作中发挥自己的优势，逐渐构建起专业的"个人品牌"，及时复盘自己每一阶段的小目标和计划，紧跟公司的发展方向，同公司共荣辱共成长。

to learn and adapt. I tell myself there is nothing to fear. In case of difficulties, the team and the company will give me a helping hand. I will speak out when I face difficulties and confusions. Communication might not necessarily solve the problems at once, but looking at problems from a different angle brings me new ideas and eliminates the risk of going into a dead end or taking a winding course. It has turned out that no matter how long the road is, we can always complete it step by step. No matter how short the road is, we will not reach it if we do not step forward. So long as we hold on to ourselves and keep faith, we will reach good results.

"Give CNOOD 10 years, and we will have a brand new self." In 2020, CNOOD will kick off a new start for the next decade. In the past six years, I have accumulated experience and have developed and transformed myself. In the next six years, I hope I will be able to take advantages of my strengths at work, build up a professional "personal brand," duly fulfill my small goals and plans at each stage, closely follow the development direction of the company and grow and prosper with the company.

张霄燕
Heather Zhang

硕士，毕业于上海对外经贸大学，2014年4月加入施璐德。
Heather graduated from the Shanghai University of International Business and Economics with a master's degree and joined CNOOD in April 2014.

心怀光明，向暖而生
With Love in Heart

■ Danni Xu

小时候，每当要求写一篇以"敬佩的人"为主题的作文时，我都会写我的妈妈。她是一名护士，在我小时候会常常值夜班，到第二天早上才会回来。在小小的我心目中，妈妈是最勤劳努力的人。

然后，一年又一年，她在这个岗位上已经坚守了35年。35年间，先后调任过外科、内科、脑外科、骨科、护理部等不同部门。我们家里人总是戏称妈妈去哪儿，哪儿就最忙。因为她天生严谨认真，到哪里都是兢兢业业、勤勤恳恳。妈妈还曾经逗我说，早知道不让你读那么多书，留在安庆给我当个小护士也不错。

When I was a pupil, I was told to write a composition on a person I admired most. I chose to write about my mother, who is a nurse. She used to work the night shift and came back home in the early morning the next day. In my little mind, she was the most diligent person in the world.

Year in and year out, Mom has worked as a nurse for 35 years. In this period, she has been shifted among the surgery, internal medicine, brain surgery, orthopedics and nursing departments. My family would joke that wherever she goes, it must be the busiest place in the hospital because we know she is rigorous and serious by nature and will work diligently in all places. She used to tease me, "If I had known earlier, I won't have let you study so hard. It will be nice to have you stay in Anqing and be a little nurse."

2019年底，妈妈依照上级安排，调任了医院新创立的院感防控及疾病控制科。不久后，新冠肺炎疫情在武汉扩散。凭借多年的护理工作经验和职业敏感，她立刻做出反应，若这场"战役"打响，院感防控科将是重要的一环。因此，她组织了一系列培训学习活动，扩充传染病防治法知识的储备，随时准备应对突发状况。

临近春节，疫情的蔓延比当初预想的还要严重，妈妈也开始了漫长的守卫战，每日早出晚归，经常深夜接到电话就出门，为了方便出门干脆直接和衣睡在沙发上。2020年1月22日，医院收治了一例新型冠状病毒肺炎的确诊病例，工作强度更大了，要分析目前现状、进一步理清流程、细致筛查感染患者、隔离传染源、督导医务人员做好防护、指导消毒等。他们像侦察兵一样穿梭于医院的每个角落，从预检分诊到发热门诊、从观察病房到隔离病区、从接收物资到医疗废物处置、从标本运送到病人转运等，所有"高风险"场所，在每一个感控环节，对每一个人员的防护，他们要做的就是牢筑遏制新冠肺炎疫情扩散的最后一道防线。每时每刻，医护人员都不能离岗。听到消息的外婆，一连几日电话询问过年我们能否回去。虽只有一小时车程，妈妈也只能遗憾说不。同样坚守在医院岗位上的还有小姨。今年我们注定不能拥有一个完美的团圆年。

At the end of 2019, Mom was transferred to the disease prevention and control section, a newly established branch of the hospital. Soon afterwards, there came the news that Wuhan had unidentified pneumonia cases. Professionally sensitive, Mom, with years of nursing experience, reacted immediately. She knew if this "battle" was to start, her section would be at the front line. She organized a series of training activities to get the staff well prepared in the knowledge of infectious disease prevention and control. They were ready to respond to emergencies.

As the Spring Festival was near, the epidemic was spreading faster than expected. Mom started her long battle against the disease. Every day, she went out early and came back late. She often went out late at night after receiving a phone call. To make it easier to go out, she slept on the couch with her clothes on. On January 22, the hospital admitted the first confirmed COVID-19 case. Mom became even busier at work. Her duty was to analyze the situation, clarify the process, screen the infected patients, isolate the sources of infection, supervise the medical personnel to get well protected and guide disinfection. Mom hustled around every corner of the hospital like a scout, involved in every link, from pre-examination and triage to the fever clinic, from observation wards to isolation wards, from supply reception to medical waste disposal, from specimen delivery to patient transport.

再后来，通过电话，我们已经很难联系上身在医院的妈妈。她直接告诉我们，不用打电话给她，有需要会联系我们。每天听到妈妈的开门声成了我和爸爸的期待。每当听到开门声，我和爸爸总会从房间的各个角落跑到门口，在距离两米的位置手舞足蹈呼喊："欢迎欢迎，热烈欢迎，英雄的母亲回来了。"这是只属于我们一家三口的仪式感。以往逢年过节回家，妈妈就像一只小蜜蜂一样，围绕着我团团转。我的妈妈一直是个乐观开朗、热情洋溢的人，只要有她在身边就会觉得很温暖。这一次，我把妈妈借给病患，让她把温暖带给更需要她的人。

疫情暴发以来，医疗物资缺乏成为一大问题。社会各界一直想方设法支援疫情防控。2月6日，在安庆市侨联的帮助下，我和校友们捐赠的消毒液成功移交到

She was present in all "high-risk" sites, in every infection control section and in the protection of every person. She built the last line of defense against the spread of COVID-19. As the situation turned serious, medical workers were told to stick to their posts. My grandma called for days in a row asking if we would go back for the Spring Festival. Although it was only an hour's drive, Mom was sorry to say no. My aunt was also fighting in her post in the hospital. So regrettably, we did not have a family reunion for the Spring Festival this year.

Later, it was hard to get in touch with Mom by phone who was in the hospital. She told us not to call her, and she would call us if anything happened. Every day, the creaky sound of door opening became what Dad and I expected most. As we heard the door open, Dad and I would run out from our rooms, dancing and shouting from two meters away, "Welcome, warmly welcome. Brave Mom has come home." It was a ritual for the three of us. In the past, when I went home on vacation for the Spring Festival and other holidays, Mom would revolve around me like a little bee. She is optimistic, cheerful and enthusiastic. As long as she is around, we feel warm at heart. This time, I lent Mom to the patients and let her bring warmth to those more in need of her.

Since the outbreak of the epidemic, the lack of medical supplies became a big problem. All sectors of the society tried every means to help epidemic prevention

医院，在物质和精神上双重支持妈妈的工作。这项工作让我知道，在这场战役中，虽然我不是前线的医护人员，但在整个人类命运共同体中，渺小如我的一点行动，或许就能为整场战役的胜利添砖加瓦。我们一家信心十足，坚信这个寒冬会很快过去。

2020年2月24日，医院的治愈比例超过80%。一名患者康复出院后说："那些说星星很亮的人，是因为没有看过护士的眼睛。"护士也只是一个个平凡的人，而每一个平凡的人，都可以燃烧自己，照

and control. On February 6, with the help of Anqing Overseas Chinese Federation, alumini from my school and I handed over donated disinfectants to the hospital to support Mom both materially and spiritually. This work let me know that in this battle, though I was not a medic on the frontline, a small action like mine could still be a little help to the victory of a battle. We are all members of a community with shared future. My family has been confident the chilly winter would be over soon.

On February 24, over 80 percent of the patients in hospital were cured. A patient discharged from the hospital after recovery said, "Those who say that stars are shining brightly haven't seen

亮别人。我们未来的路还很长，但只要内心光芒万丈，就不怕暂时的黑夜与悲伤，既能扛起眼前的苟且，也能眺望诗和远方。

the nurses' eyes." Nurses are ordinary people, but ordinary people can also burn themselves to illuminate others. We have a long way to go, but as long as we have rays of light in our hearts, we won't fear temporary night and sorrow. We will be able to drift along at the moment and look forward to a brighter future.

徐丹妮
Danni Xu

2016年4月正式加入施璐德，成为公司投融资部的一名成员。渴望拥吃喝玩乐的生活和充实的精神世界，并为此不懈努力。

Danni formally joined CNOOD in April 2016 and became a member of the investment and financing department. She longs to have an enjoyable material life and an affluent spiritual life and is making unremitting efforts to achieve these.

不一样的春节

An Unusual Spring Festival

■ Jenna Hu

2020年的春节，注定是一个不平凡的春节，这个春节没有了以往熙熙攘攘的大街，少了走亲访友的聚会，但也多了很多不同的感受。

自豪

新冠肺炎疫情的暴发，牵动着每一个中国人的心。每天醒来的第一件事就是看新增的确诊病例，祈祷那根增长曲线可以放缓，可以早日下降。数据表里最扎眼的当数死亡人数，它不是一个个冷冰冰的数据，死亡人数背后是一个个破碎的家庭。北野武的那句话直击人心，他说：什么是灾难？灾难并不是死了两万人这样一件事，而是死了一个人这件事，发生了两万次。

为了解决患者的床位问题，尽早集中

The Spring Festival of 2020 was quite uncommon. It went without the traditional bustling streets or lively gatherings of relatives and friends. However, it also left us with a lot of unusual feelings.

Pride

The outbreak of the COVID-19 epidemic shook every Chinese. The first thing I would check in the morning was the updates of new confirmed cases. I prayed that the growth curve could become flattened earlier. The most eye-catching part of the data sheet was the number of deaths. It was not a cold figure, for behind the death toll were numerous broken families. At that moment, I thought of a remark by Takeshi Kitano: What is a disaster? A disaster is not the death of 20,000 people. It is death happening 20,000 times.

To supply more sickbeds to treat

收治新冠肺炎患者，武汉参照2003年抗击非典期间北京小汤山医院模式，建设了火神山、雷神山两家医院。火神山医院从方案设计到建成交付，只用了10天时间，中国再次向世界展现了中国速度。从电视里看到整个建造过程的快速推进时，油然而生的是对祖国强大的自豪感，同时产生的还有作为一名工程人的自信和使命感。其实，身为一名工程人才知道这背后有多么不容易，大家眼中的奇迹，是7 000多名建设者日夜鏖战的成果，中国速度是患难与共、众志成城的信仰。正所谓：哪有什么基建狂魔，都是血肉之躯用生命筑成的堡垒。

COVID-19 patients in a centralized way, Wuhan followed the model of Beijing Xiaotangshan Hospital in the fight against SARS in 2003. It hence built two makeshift hospitals, by the name of Huoshenshan and Leishenshan. It took only 10 days to complete the Huoshenshan Hospital, from project design to construction and to delivery. It showed once again the China speed. As I watched video clips of the entire construction process on TV, a sense of pride welled up in my heart eulogizing the power of my motherland. I was also hit by a sense of confidence and mission as an engineer. I knew how hard it was to work the miracle, as more than 7,000 builders dedicated themselves day and night. The China speed was a belief to share weal and woe and unite as one. The builders were not maniacs, but loyal soldiers constructing the life-saving fortress with flesh and blood.

感动

由于新冠肺炎疫情的暴发，为了控制疫情扩散，各市之间，各个小区，各个村庄都设置了很多卡点，对过往的车辆以及行人进行健康检查。其间，很多人放弃了春节假期，放弃了与家人团聚的时间，走上了特殊的工作岗位。

坐高铁要到隔壁市，这条路已经走过了很多遍，但这次的出行是从来没有过的体验。一路上，路上的车辆比平时少了很多，几乎见不到行人，大家都在响应号召，居家隔离。到了两市的交界处，看到了卡点，亲眼见到了奋战在一线的工作人

Moved

To contain the spread of the epidemic, many health check points were set up at entrances to communities and villages across the country. Many people gave up their Spring Festival holidays and family reunions to work at the special new posts.

I have travelled many times to the neighboring city by high-speed trains. This time, I made the trip by car and had an unprecedented experience. Along the highway, I saw fewer cars than usual days and even fewer pedestrians. Everyone

员。道路旁搭了好几个临时的棚子，放着登记用的桌椅、测温用的仪器。工作人员有的负责引导，有的负责记录，有的负责测体温，现场有条不紊。为了减少大家等待的时间，同时也是防止人员聚集，现场用的是红外测温，只需摇下车窗，车内的人都看着探头，就能对车内的人一起测温，方便快捷，又无接触，不得不感叹如今科技的发展。由于防护服紧缺，有的工作人员穿的是一次性雨衣。离开的时候由衷地向他们说了声谢谢，虽然隔着口罩，看不到大家的脸，但是口罩隔离的是病毒，隔离不了爱。

后来在公众号上看到的消息更让人动

stayed at home for self quarantine in response to the government's call. At the junction where the two cities met, I saw a check point and workers on duty there. A few temporary sheds were erected by the roadside, with tables and chairs for registration and with instruments for measuring temperature. Some people were busy guiding the way, while others kept records and measured body temperature. They were busy but in an orderly way. To shorten our waiting time and keep distance, infrared temperature measurement devices were adopted on the site. This way, drivers only needed to roll down car windows and look at the camera to have their temperature measured, which proved convenient, fast and without contact. How I marvelled at today's technology. As protective suits fell short, some wore disposable raincoats for protection. When I drove away, I shouted my thanks to them. We wore facial masks and could not see each other's face, but they only blocked virus, not our mutual love.

容，虽然只是几个记录现场的短视频。由于冷空气来袭，同时还带来了降雨，大风吹跑了卡点的棚子，工作人员有的冒雨抢修，有的坚守岗位，对过往车辆人员进行引导、检查、记录。看着视频，心里满是感动，这是冬日雨夜带给人的温暖，带给人的力量，正印证了那句话：哪有什么岁月静好，不过是有人替你负重前行。

Later, I saw some touching on-the-spot video clips on WeChat. The cold air blasted, bringing rain and gale that blew away the hut at the check spot. Some staff rushed to repair the hut in the rain, while others stuck to their posts to guide, check and record each passing vehicle and person. I felt an upsurge of emotions on that rainy winter night. It verified the catchwords: We enjoy quiet good years only because some others are carrying the load for us.

希望

经过全国人民的努力，疫情得到了有效控制，寒冬已过，春天如期到来。春暖花开，万物复苏，企业已经陆续复工，生活慢慢回到正轨，但大家都没放松警惕，做好体温监测，做到不扎堆，不接触。马路上，行人变多了，但大家都自觉地戴着口罩，是对自己的保护，更是对他人的尊重。经过大家不懈的努力，我们终将等到摘下口罩的那天，再次看到大家绽放笑容的脸。

2020年有一个不一样的开端，但只要我们砥砺前行，2020年也必将成为精彩的一年。

Hope

Thanks to the concerted efforts of the Chinese people, the epidemic is effectively controlled in China. Now, the chilly winter has passed, and the warm spring has come around. When spring blossoms, everything comes back to life. Enterprises have started to resume production. Life is on the way to return to normal. We remain alert, take temperature screening and keep social distance. Anyway, there are more pedestrians on the roads. Everyone is still wearing facial masks to protect themselves and show respect to others. With unremitting efforts of everyone, we will have the day when we take off facial masks and see smiling faces again.

The year 2020 started in an unusual way. As long as we forge ahead, we can make it a wonderful year in the end.

胡静航
Jenna Hu

2015年6月毕业于复旦大学材料科学系，2015年7月正式加入CNOOD，成为人生中第一份工作。脚踏实地、仰望星空是之前学习和现在工作中的座右铭。

Jenna graduated from the Department of Materials Science, Fudan University in June 2015 and joined CNOOD in July of the same year to have the first job in her lifetime. "Plant your feet firmly on the ground and look up at the stars" is her motto both in college and at work.

娱乐至死

Amusing Ourselves to Death

■ Johnson Shen

奥威尔担心我们憎恨的东西会毁掉我们，而赫胥黎担心的是，我们将毁于我们热爱的东西。印刷时代造就了理性思辨的人，电视时代造就了娱乐至死的人。媒介通过一种潜移默化的隐形力量，塑造着人类的认知。

在 19 世纪，印刷时代造就了理性思辨的美国人，按照波兹曼的说法，这和阅读文化息息相关，因为文字本身就非常适合传递思辨性的观点。不过，电视则恰恰相反，这种媒介技术并不适合严肃的逻辑思考，电视上每个镜头的平均时间只有 3.5 秒，充满了视觉的刺激、动态的切换。因此，波兹曼非常不屑地吐槽说：在电视上，复杂的措辞、充分的证据和逻辑都派不上用场，有时候连句法也被丢到一边，但这并没有什么关系，政治家们关心的是给观众留下印象，而不是给观众留下观点。在他的年代，电视机的出现开始对我们的生活产生巨大变化，媒体的传播途径变得开阔和便捷，不像以前那样只能通

George Orwell feared that what we hate would destroy us. Aldous Leonard Huxley worried that we would be ruined by what we love. The printing age produced rational thinkers, and the television age made people entertain to death. The media has shaped human cognition through subtle invisible forces.

In the 19th century, the printing age created rational, speculative Americans. As Neil Postman put it, this is closely related to the reading culture, because words are perfect for conveying speculative ideas. However, televisions are the opposite. This media technology is not fit for serious logical thinking. The average time per shot on television is only 3.5 seconds, full of visual stimuli and dynamic switching. So Postman said with great disdain: On TV, complicated diction, sufficient evidence and logic are useless. Sometimes, even syntax is thrown aside. However, it doesn't matter. Politicians care to impress

过报纸或电报。这种速度上的推进使我们更快速地接触每一步信息,而电视为了吸引人,自然不会以传统的教书似的方式进行沟通,娱乐化的模式便出现了。

文学、宗教、音乐等都希望借助这样一个便捷的工具来推进,而找到一个让普通人也能接受的途径,娱乐的方式解决了这个问题。在这种现象的初期,我想是有意义的,那个时代的人们并没有太多机会了解更多的知识,电视节目的娱乐性也会体现出它的价值。波兹曼认为,电视特别适合做娱乐节目。所以说,娱乐其实是电视的最佳用途。

the audience, not to leave them a point of view. In his time, TV sets emerged to make great changes in people's lives. Media's channels of communication became extensive and convenient, not confined to newspapers and telegrams as before. This improved speed allowed us to get in touch with information at each step more quickly. To attract the audience, TV programs naturally did not communicate in the traditional way of teaching. So the pattern of entertainment emerged.

Literature, religion and music want to advance with such a convenient tool and find a way to be accepted by ordinary people. Entertainment has solved the problem. I think it was of significance in the early days of this phenomenon. People of that era did not have much opportunity to learn more knowledge, and the entertainment of television had its value. Postman thought that television wass especially suitable for entertainment programs. Thus, entertainment is actually the best use of television.

可后续的发展却不是那么回事，不仅是那些打发时间的，连一些真正渴望知识的也习惯于去电视节目中学习。那这样真的好吗？当然，我不能否认电视节目中不可能什么知识也没有，问题只在于它的表达方式上，它太过于附和普通人的心理需求了，也就是说太过盲目和附庸了。如果我们用电视来思考严肃的政治信息，就会变成娱乐至死的物种。书中说到这么一句：文化将成为一场滑稽戏，等待我们的可能是一个娱乐至死的"美丽新世界"，在那里"人们感到痛苦的不是他们用笑声代替了思考，而是他们不知道自己为什么笑以及为什么不再思考"。

But that's not what happened next. Not only those who wanted to pass the time but also some of those who were really thirst for knowledge had got used to studying on TV. Is that really good? Of course, I can't claim there's no knowledge on TV. The problem is simply with its way of expression, which is too accommodating to the psychological needs of ordinary people, that is, too blind and obedient. If we use TV as the tool to ponder over serious political information, we will become a species of entertainment to death. The book noted that culture would be a farce, and what awaited us might be a "brave new world" of entertainment to death, where "what makes people miserable is not that they laugh instead of thinking but that they don't know why they laugh and why they don't think any more".

这样的结果让人感到害怕，莺歌燕舞中的芸芸众生只是为了娱乐而娱乐，而对于如何生成一套解释和认知世界的理论，娱乐无能为力。当世界在黑暗的语境中难得地安静下来时，焦虑和无力感将如鼠疫一样蔓延，只有当下一次娱乐狂欢降临，人群才会告别墓地般的安静，这种恶性循环已经成为一种稳定的机制，也是我们时代病灶所在。我们依从于一种不知为何的行为，却不明何以为之，甚至都不愿思之。这样的文化传递方式正在改变我们的生活。

在波兹曼的时代，电脑还没有像今天这样在我们的日常生活中无可替代，但他也已对可以预见的电脑时代提出了警告，而今日的事实比他猜想的更让人悲观。当

Such a result is frightening. The myriad beings enjoy the joys of life just for the fun. There is nothing entertainment can do about generating a set of theories to explain and recognize the world. When the world has a rare moment of quieting down in a dark context, anxiety and powerlessness will spread like plague. Only when the next carnival of entertainment falls will the crowd bid farewell to the grave-like silence. This vicious circle has become a stable mechanism and the focus of infection of our time. We rely on an inexplicable behavior but don't know why, and we don't even want to think about it. Such a way of cultural transmission is changing our lives.

In Postman's time, computers were not as irreplaceable in daily lives as they are today, but he still warned about the foreseeable computer age. Today's facts

下，我们被淹没在各种电子信息中，不论电子产品以怎样的形式被发明，它的演绎方式始终没有变，总是习惯于把娱乐性放在第一位，互联网最大的问题之一，便是让我们失去了阅读和思考的耐心。

为什么害怕，并不是认为娱乐会让我们腐化，而是我们太简单地用娱乐去考虑每一件事情，或者连思考都放弃了。

are more pessimistic than he suspected. We are now submerged in all kinds of electronic information. No matter how electronic products were invented, their path for development has never changed, as they have always put entertainment first. One of the biggest problems of the Internet is that it let us lose the patience of reading and thinking.

Why are we afraid? It is not that entertainment will corrupt us but that we simply think of everything as entertainment or even give up the entertainment of thinking.

沈佳祺
Johnson Shen

所有的相遇，都是久别重逢。不知不觉在 CNOOD 已经六年多了。在这样一个关怀他人、提升自我的集体中，始终能让自己充满正能量。走遍世界的角落，带着自由而无用的灵魂。

Every occasion of encounter is a reunion after a long separation. I have been working at CNOOD for more than six years before I know it. I am always filled with positive energy in such a mutually caring and self-promoting organization. With a free and useless soul, I'm going across every corner of the world.

迟来的一封告别信
A Late Farewell Letter

■ Loreen Luo

时间真的过得好快，转眼就来到2020年3月，距我离开CNOOD这个大家庭，已经整整两年了。记得2018年的4月1日晚上，收拾整理好自己所有的私人物品，离开了人生中的第一份工作，离开了一起相处快五年的同事们。心里好像突然空了一大块，五味杂陈，好像有很多的话想说，很多的人想告别，却又不知从何说起。后来索性一句话都没说，一个人也没去告别，而是最后一次在公司的定位上发了一条朋友圈——汪峰的一首歌《再见青春》。是啊，原来在过去的五年，CNOOD不仅是一份工作，更是我五年的青春呀，与同学和同事们一起奋斗成长的青春岁月。工作可能会有第二个五年，第三个五年……可是一起奋斗、全情投入的青春岁月，只有一次。所以，写一封和大家的告别信，对于当时的我来说真的很难提笔，只想逃避，不去面对。没想到这一拖欠，就是两年。两年时间说长不长，说短也不短，但却足以能够让我跳出两年前迫切想离开的心态和状态，跳出当时自己的情绪，客观地感受和体会在CNOOD这

Time really flies. In the twinkling of an eye, it is now March 2020 already. It has been two years since I left the big family of CNOOD. I still remember that on the evening of April 1, 2018, I packed all my personal belongings to leave the first job in my life and to leave the colleagues I had worked with for nearly five years. Suddenly I had mixed feelings as if having a big hole in my heart. There seemed to be a lot to say and a lot of people to say goodbye to, but I did not know where to start. So I didn't say any word or say goodbye to anyone. Instead, I posted for the last time at CNOOD's office location a song of Wang Feng—*Goodbye to Youth*—on my WeChat Moments. Yes, it turned out that in the past five years, CNOOD not only provided a job for me but also represented 5 years of my youth, the youthful days of struggling along with colleagues. We may have the second five

五年来的经历和成长，借此封迟来的告别信分享给大家。想了很久，想梳理一个合适的思路来表达，脑海里浮现了曾经在环球世界大厦10楼办公室的小会议室里，我与老池辩论的情景（关于公司的文化、制度和业务方向等），那就用2018年离开时的Loreen与2020年此刻的Loreen一问一答的形式来展开吧。

1. 为什么在CNOOD总是有一些和工作不直接相关的"杂事"要做？

可能很多同事都有过同样的感受，这件事情明明和我要从事的工作不相关，为什么我总是要去做，感觉像打杂。比如举办年会，为什么不是行政部来做；比如招聘，为什么不是人事部来做；比如组织、参加公司对外的分享和活动，这又跟我的工作有什么关系；比如装修办公室，这耽误报价和做项目；比如从智利购买车厘子，这个项目没有提成；比如筹备开个饭

years, the third five years at work, but we would have only one youth when we were fully devoted and struggled together. Thus, it was really difficult for me at that time to write a farewell letter to everyone, as I just wanted to escape rather than to face. I didn't expect this delay to last two years. Two years are neither long nor short, but they are enough to get me out of the state of mind of two years ago when I was eager to leave. Now I've got out of the mood of that time and can objectively reflect on my experience and growth at CNOOD over the five years. I'd like to share them in this late farewell letter with you. I've thought about it for a long time, trying to sort out a suitable idea to express myself. What came to my mind were the scenes of arguing with Dennis over corporate culture, institutions and business directions in the small conference room on the 10th floor of Universal Mansion. So let's start with a dialogue between the Loreen leaving in 2018 and the Loreen today.

1. Why should I do "chores" at CNOOD that are unrelated to my job?

Many colleagues might have felt the same way: This work is clearly unrelated to my job, and so why should I always have to do it, as if I were a do-all? For example, why is it not the administration department who organize the annual meeting? Why is it not the human resources department who arrange the recruitment? Why should I participate

店，这跟我们业务差距太大了；比如帮同事在1个月内办场婚礼，这跟本职工作差距太远了吧；等等。这些和工作岗位内容不相关，且费时费力，耽误"正经"工作。现在终于能够理解老池的那句老生常谈的话："通过做好一件事，什么事情都能拿得起，放得下。你会剥香蕉吃，你就可以做好项目。"这些打杂的事，要做好，都需要一个全面的思路去考量问题，良好的沟通和心态去协调人员。可并不是每个人都能这么幸运，有这么多"打杂"的事情去积累经验，在大部分公司，每个人都只能做自己岗位的事情，看到自己岗位可以看到的东西，不同办公室的门是紧闭的，公司的系统是严格规定权限的，会议室是十分私密的，去考察看厂，拜访客户可以一个人去，就绝对不要两个人去的（出于成本和岗位工作范围的考量）。没有机会真正地看清自己在做事情的全貌，也没有太多机会接触和学习，当要独当一面的时候，完全找不到正确的思路。"打杂"让我们长见识，培养解决问题的思路和承受力，心里不慌了，思路是对的，事情都会解决。你之所以可以承担起这个责任，解决好这些问题，不是与生俱来，而是你有机会经历过。

in the sharing activities with other companies? They have nothing to do with my job. The decoration of the office delays my quotation work and project participation. There is no commission for me to buy cherries from Chile. Planning to open a restaurant has little to do with our business. Helping to hold a colleague's wedding in a month is far from my own duty. All these issues are unrelated to my post, wasting my time and energy and delaying my "serious" work. Now I can finally understand what Dennis often said, "By doing one thing well, you can pick up anything and do it well. If you can peel the banana, you can do the project well." To do the "chores" well, we need a holistic approach to consider issues and good communication skills and attitude to coordinate with others. Not everyone is so lucky to have so many "chores" to accumulate experience. In most companies, staff can only do their own jobs and see what they can see in their positions. The doors of offices are closed. The company's system is strictly regulated. The meeting rooms are very private. If one person can do it to visit a factory or a customer alone, it is not be necessary to send two people, due to considerations of costs and scopes of duty. If we do not have the chance to see the whole picture of what we are doing in concrete-or the opportunity to socialize and learn, we will not know which way to think when we are to work alone. Doing "chores" gives us increasing insights and

（自我体会案例：2019年帮现在公司筹办两场很仓促的行业展会，在零基础上，一场用了2周准备，另一场准备时间只有3天，老板再三和我确认怕我这边准备不了，但是我心里还是有把握，没有问题，这是我的强项。因为曾经在CNOOD主要承办过德国展会和其他很多会议，公司每次的宣传册制作我都有参与，因此整个展会流程、宣传资料对我来说都不是问题，结果展会举办很成功。2018年11月—2019年4月，和现在公司的老板一起去湖南建了一个复合材料工厂，从零开始，在公司注册、网站、宣传册、招聘、装修、设备购买、安装等各个环节，都基本独当一面。可是我心里很清楚，这些经验的积累，都是CNOOD赋予我的，放手让你去做，充分的信任，甚至不计成本的成全。）

develops the ideas and capacity for solving problems. When we don't panic and have the right ideas, everything will work out. We can take up the responsibility and solve the problems, not because we were born with the capacity but because we had a chance to experience them.

(My experience: In 2019, I was entrusted by my current company to organize two trade shows in a hurry. Starting from scratch, I spent two weeks to prepare for one and only three days for the other. The boss asked me time and again, fearing I could not do it. However, I was still confident, as it was my strength. When I was at CNOOD, I organized exhibitions in Germany and many other meetings. I was involved in preparing all the brochures. So I was quite familiar with the exhibition process and publicity material preparations. The events turned out to be great success. From November 2018 to April 2019, I assisted the boss of my current company to build a composite material factory in Hunan. We started empty-handed. I took charge of many procedures independently, including company registration, website construction, brochure production, recruitment, factory decoration, equipment purchase and installation. I knew in my heart that all these accumulated experiences were given by CNOOD. CNOOD just let me do it at my own pace, granted me full trust and helped me to complete tasks even regardless of costs.)

2. 为什么公司的业务和项目方向总是在变动?

这个问题,就是我当年在环球世界大厦10楼和老池辩论的问题之一。当时我是这么问的:"为什么我过去一年都是在做油套管项目,可是今年接触的都是管桩项目,还要弄风电,要做EPC?我油套管都还没学会学精呢,总是在做不熟悉的项目,那我们是不是还要做神舟五号啊?为什么不专注在某一两个类型?"老池是这么回答的:"我们没有选择的权力,我们要在市场上活下来,就要顺应市场去变。"是啊,要活下来。只有一直走在市场前面,走在客户一线的人,才知道市场需要什么,客户在找什么,客户的要求和预算是多少。提供客户想要的东西,我们才能活下来,活得好。CNOOD不是卖钢管的,是做项目的,培养的不是业务员,出售的不是产品,而是培养项目管理团队,出售的是项目管理价值。

(自我体会案例:在展会上结识了一个上市公司专门做生物医疗设备的客户,他们首席技术总监跟我说:"小罗,我们别的供应商都觉得我们很难搞,要求多,但是我觉得你一点都不嫌我们麻烦、要求

2. Why are the business and project directions of CNOOD always changing?

This is one of the issues I argued with Dennis on the 10th floor of Universal Mansion in those years. Here's what I asked, "How come I've been working on the oil casing project in the past year but was shifted to the piling pipe, wind power and EPC projects this year? I haven't mastered the oil casing knowledge yet, and I am always working on unfamiliar projects. Are we also going to launch the Shenzhou V spacecraft? Why not focus on one or two business models?" Dennis replied, "We have no choice. We must adapt to the market if we want to survive in the market." That's true. We have to survive first. Only those who keep ahead of the market and keep contact with customers in the front line know what the market needs, what the customers are looking for, what the customers require and how much their budgets are. Only by providing what the customers want can we survive and live well. CNOOD is not selling steel pipes but working on projects. It is not training salespersons or selling products but training project management teams and selling the value of project management.

(My experience: I met a client from a listed company specializing in biomedical equipment at a fair. The CTO of the company told me, "Loreen, other suppliers of ours complain that

高啊。"在实践的接触中发现，真正落实全程第三方质检，产前会确认所有的检验计划、过程文件、MRB 等详细质控流程和技术文件，除了 CNOOD 真的可能找不出第二家了。用 CNOOD 的标准去对待现在的客户，都能获得好评，难就难在要说服公司很多其他的同事来配合，因为大家对质量控制和项目管理的意识大相径庭。）

we are hard to deal with, as we raise a lot of requirements. I've found that you are different, as you don't mind we raise so many high requirements." In practice, I've found that only CNOOD truly implemented the third party quality inspection in the whole process and confirmed all inspection plans, process documents, Material Review Board (MRB) and other detailed quality control procedures and technical documents before production. Handling customers with the CNOOD standard, we will surely win good comments. The only problem is convincing other colleagues in the company to cooperate and follow the same procedure, as they have different views on quality control and project management.)

3. 为什么感觉不公平，明明差不多时间进来的人，收入差距可能很大？

这个问题曾经困扰过我，相信也困扰过很多其他同事。其实这个和第二个问题的本质原因是一致的。老池创立 CNOOD 的"发心"是创建一个平台，让志同道合的人能一起在这个平台上相互成全、相互成就。大部分人创办公司的目的，是通过雇佣员工，组合团队，来让自己赚钱。相信每一个 CNOOD 人，都知道老池他到底赚不赚钱，有没有"榨取"员工创造的价值。答案是十分明确和简单的，老池只赚自己的业务提成，从来不榨取别人创造的价值，反而还要把自己的提成拿到公司来搞活动，开年会，补贴公司家用。CNOOD 提供一个平台，这个平台

3. Why do you feel unfair, as people admitted at about the same time may have a big income gap?

I used to be bothered by this issue, and I believe it is true with many of my colleagues. In fact, it is consistent in nature with the second problem. Dennis founded CNOOD for the purpose of creating a platform where like-minded people can work together to achieve common success. Most people start a company to make money by hiring people and building teams. I'm sure every CNOOD member knows whether Dennis makes money or "squeezes" the value of employees. The answer is clear and simple. Dennis only earns his own

上有土壤、空气、水，让每颗种子自己发芽成长。公司会分享很多的客户和项目资源，可是这些仅仅是机会，而不是直接的订单。哪些客户好，哪些单会成，这些都是要去做了，才能知道的，公司也是在市场的海浪中翻滚、沉浮，接受考验，却无法预知结果。CNOOD可以做到的公平，是这个平台机制的公平，每个人都有均等的参与机会，每个人所参与的规则是统一的，分配制度不因人而异。坦诚说，付出努力，没赚到相应的钱，心里肯定是难过的，可是人生就是这样，很多时候金钱回报和付出并不是一一对等，但并不代表失败和一无所获。

（自我体会案例：在CNOOD的薪酬制度都是公开透明的，而在很多公司觉得公开薪酬简直是完全不敢想象的事情，同岗不同酬的事情经常发生。结果是，每个人都觉得自己的工资是不是比同事低，抱怨是常有的事。在这两年中，因巧合结识了很多在杨浦科创中心的年轻创业者，他们都怀有梦想，十分努力，时常都是工作到深夜。可是真正创业成功的在极少数，

business commission and never extracts the value created by others. Instead, he uses his own commission to organize company activities, hold annual meetings and subsidize the company's daily expenses. CNOOD provides a platform with soil, air and water so that each seed can germinate and grow by itself. The company shares a lot of customer information and project resources, which are opportunities only, rather than direct orders. Only after following these opportunities closely can we know which opportunities are finally going to be orders. The company is like a boat rolling and fluctuating in the waves of the market under tests, but the results are unpredictable. The fairness that CNOOD can prolide is the fairness of the mechanism of the platform where everyone has an equal opportunity to participate under unified rules and a fair distribution system. To be honest, it must be sad to work hard without due returns. However, this is life. On many occasions, we do not necessarily gain adequate rewards for our efforts, but it does not mean failure or completely no gains.

(My experience: At CNOOD, the payment system is open and transparent. In many companies, disclosure of payment is completely unimaginable. Unequal pay for the same job often happens. As a result, everyone feels that he is paid less than others, and they often complain. Over the past two years, I happened to meet some young

要么遇到资金瓶颈,要么遇到发展瓶颈。有些迫于生活的压力,不得不放下自己手头的项目,去找工作了。而有的在多次失败经验的积累下,一下子就出来了。其实,把自己当作一个创业者,不是每一次机会都能赢,但经历了,总有一天会豁然开朗的。)

4. 为什么老池总是喜欢搞分享,搞CNOOD学会这种"务虚"的?

两年没有"务虚"了,突然感觉灵魂有点枯竭,感觉自己一直在输出,而没有输入。成长最快的方法,就是跟对的人去学。分享让每一个单一的个体,有机会进行融会贯通。现在很流行一句话:"分享即链接,付出即收获"。如果一个公司的每个人只埋头在自己的半平方米工位,不关心别人在做什么,甚至想保留自己的技能和经验,以获得自己在公司存在的价值,这样的工作是很压抑的,成长也是最慢的。没有交流,就没有碰撞,就没有更好的解决方案。不沟通,就会发生大问题。老池时常和大家务虚,谈他的观点,希望我们充分表达自己的看法,甚至每次都讲一样的主题,重复反复讲。我想他是希望我们能够真正地用心去体会和理解吧,只有我们真正地去体会、理解了,才能融合在我们的处事为人中,形成CNOOD独有的文化,才能去传承。"爱文化""家文化""100%尊重""100%透

entrepreneurs at Yangpu Science and Innovation Centre. With dreams in head, they work hard and often late into the night, but few have achieved success, as they encountered either fund shortage or development bottlenecks. Under the pressure of life, some had to drop their projects and find jobs. Some others succeeded after experiencing many failures. In fact, as entrepreneurs, it is impossible for us to win in every opportunity, but having experienced so much, there will always be a day when everything is suddenly enlightened.)

4. Why is Dennis fond of sharing and "discussing principles"?

It has been two years that I have not discussed "principles." Suddenly I feel my soul is a little bit exhausted, and I was giving outputs all the time without any input gained. The fastest way to grow is to learn from the right person. Sharing gives an individual the opportunity to put it all together. The concept that "Sharing is linking, and giving is gaining" is very popular now. If everyone in a company only buries themselves into their own seats in office, does not care what others are doing or even wants to retain their own skills and experience to acquire his value of existence in the company, under such circumstances, the work must be depressing, and people with such idea are definitely those who grow at the the slowest pace. Without communication, there will be no collision

明""100% 信任",这些虽然还是让很多人觉得很虚,但是已经有很多 CNOOD 人从中受益。此处我就不列举了,大家可以自行体会一下,受到过老池和 CNOOD 的特殊的超过自己期待的关爱,超出利益和雇佣合同义务的关爱,这只有来自家人和挚友。我之前也不是那么理解,CNOOD 为什么每年都要出年鉴。现在看来,出年鉴,以书的形式记录公司每一个同事的分享和成长经历,就能无限和重复地传播出去,而不受制于时间和空间,公司的文化就可以很好地吸引、凝聚到同频的人。

of thoughts, let alone better solutions. Without communication, big problems may emerge. Dennis often discusses principles with his staff and expresses his views, hoping that we can also fully express our own. He would talk about the same topic every time, repeating it over and over again. I think what he really wants is to let us experience and understand things sincerely. Only when we have truly experienced and understood it can we integrate it into our conduct and form the unique culture of CNOOD and pass it on. The "culture of love" "culture of family" "100% respect" "100% transparency" and "100% trust" — although many people consider these as mere empty words, actually many people at CNOOD are benefitting from them. I won't list these in too much detail. We may experience ourselves how the care and love from Dennis and CNOOD goes beyond our expectations. Such care is beyond benefits and contractual obligations, which only comes from our families and close friends. I didn't understand it before why CNOOD compiled the yearbook. I felt that it costed a lot, and it actually did as I'm very clear about the expenses. Now it seems that publishing the yearbook by sharing the growth experience of every colleague in the company, the corporate culture can be repeated, and it spreads out without constraint of time and space. By doing so, like-minded people are attracted to come and join in.

（自我体会案例：时常，酸奶、可乐、冰棒堆满冰箱，公司发放或提供各种节日购物卡、年终爱心奖、考证学习基金、超长蜜月游、病假，手机屏幕裂了被送一个新的，电脑卡顿了被送一台新的，家里有好事、难事公司背后的支持，最关键的是平等尊重每一个人的想法，尊重每一个人的表达权，可以自由参加任何自己想参加的会议，和现在的同事聊天才发现这些都是那么的不可思议。这些都是在他们以往经历的任何一个公司都不曾有过的。有时候，我也经常跟他们聊聊老池和公司一些同事的"奇闻轶事"，他们都很羡慕一毕业就能有机会进CNOOD的人。）

5. 老池是不是膨胀了，为什么办公室要越换越大，越换越好？

稍微来得久一点的同事，都知道CNOOD搬过四次家。从以前环球世界大厦很小的7楼，到自己刷墙并与口腔诊所各半的10楼，再到用心斥资装修的整层9楼，再到越商大厦的8楼。其间的租金、物业费和装修费都增加了不少，记得那时候会觉得老池是不是膨胀了，为啥要租那么大的办公室，还要装修。除了员工逐渐增加这个原因，好的办公环境，能让大家身心愉快，让生活和工作都能更加体面，

(My experience: The fridge of CNOOD is often packed with yogurt, cola and popsicles. CNOOD provides shopping cards for holidays, annual bonuses, certificates and education funds, super long honeymoon holidays and sick leave. You get a new phone when the old one has a screen crack. You get a new computer when the old one runs too slow. You have the support of the company when something very happy or difficult happens in your family. Most importantly, everyone's idea is treated equally, and everyone's right of expression is respected. You can freely attend any meeting we are interested in. As I chat with my colleagues now, I find these are incredible in other places. They have never experienced such things in other companies. Sometimes, I tell them the "anecdotes" of Dennis and my previous colleagues. Having entered CNOOD directly after graduation draws the envy of my current colleagues.)

5. Is Dennis complacent? Why does he change for bigger and better offices?

Staff having worked at CNOOD for a longer period know that the company has moved four times. It started in a small space on the 7th floor of Universal Mansion; then it was moved to the shabby office adjacent to a dental clinic on the 10th floor , then to the whole 9th floor with refined decoration and finally to the 8th floor of Yueshang Plaza. Thus, the rent, property management fees and

谁不愿意过着有尊严更体面的生活呢？大多数老板是拿赚的钱去给自己买更大更多的房子，更奢华的装修，更多的去节约公司运营成本，可老池完全是反其道而行。这背后，是对CNOOD所有家人的关爱，这是我现在的体会。

（自我体会案例：原来有一种装修叫老板办公室装修，就是老板的办公室装修得极度豪华，私密性强，主要领导办公室次豪华，其他统一简装隔间，相信大家也去过不少有类似情况的公司吧。）

6. 感觉工作压力比较大，时常感到迷茫，工作量也大，为什么不能朝九晚五？

直白说，CNOOD是属于奋斗者的，喜欢"钱多、事少、离家近"和喜欢"钱少、事少、离家近"的人都不太适合CNOOD的工作。CNOOD所做的工作就是很多公司做不好、不愿做，严格、严

decoration expenses have increased a lot. I was wondering whether Dennis might begin to be complacent. If not, why did he rent such a big office with refined decorations? It turned out that in addition to accommodating the increasing numbers of staff, he believed that a good office environment would make everyone happy. It provides us an environment to live and work in a decent way. Anyway, who doesn't want to live a decent life with dignity? Most bosses would spend the money they earn to buy more and bigger luxurious houses, and they would manage to cut down the company's operating costs. Dennis does exactly the opposite. Behind the moves are his concern for all CNOOD members. This is what I'm thinking now.

(My experience: The decorations of the offices for bosses are typical in that the decorations are always luxurious and greatly emphasizing privacy. The offices of the main leaders are inferior. Others are simply decorated office cubicles. I'm sure you've been to a lot of such companies.)

6. I feel that the work pressure is very big and often get lost under the heavy workload. Why can't I work by the traditional nine to five routine?

Frankly speaking, CNOOD is a company for striving entrepreneurs. Those who like "more salary, less work and closer to home" and those who prefer "less salary, less work and closer

格、再严格，一定程度"反人性"的工作。因此超强的责任心，解决头疼的难题，细致跟踪是完成好项目的必备。做不容易做的事情，当然会累和有压力，时刻不能掉以轻心。曾经自己在工作迷茫时候很懊恼，总想跳出所处的困境，逃离出去，觉得离开了就是出口。现在回过头来看，在哪工作都会迷茫，只要在做开创性的工作，都会迷茫，换哪一家公司都一样。关键是要坚持做，总会熬过去。是的，坚持去做，去改善，时间会解决一切问题。曾经自己也很羡慕能够朝九晚五的公司，现在才意识到朝九晚五也意味着没有自由。在CNOOD，每个人可以根据自己的客户和项目，根据具体情况的要求，去完成好工作就行，把一切形式主义降到最低。工作日也不是不可以去迪士尼，错峰旅游、回家也是自由的。拥有早上8点收到客户邮件可以选择第一时间在家处理，而不是先不处理，赶紧出门到公司打卡的自由。

to home" are not suitable to work at CNOOD. At CNOOD, you are engaged in works that many companies do not do or cannot do well. The works are strict, and to some extent "against human nature." Therefore, a strong sense of responsibility, the capacity to solve knotty problems and meticulous tracking are necessary for completing projects well. It is naturally tiresome and stressed to do a hard job, but we should never take things lightly. Once, I was annoyed when I was confused at work. I wanted to jump out of the predicament and even to escape from it, feeling that to leave was the exit of the situation. Now when I look back into those days, I find that we may feel confused wherever we work. As long as the work we're doing is pioneering, we may get lost in any company. The key is to persist in doing it, and we'll get through it finally. For sure, keep doing it and making improvement, and all problems shall be solved as time goes by. I once envied the traditional nine to five routine jobs. Now what I realize is that the nine-to-five jobs do not mean freedom either. At CNOOD, everyone can schedule their works and get them done according to the specific requirements of customers and projects. It reduces all forms of formalities. It's not impossible to go to Disneyland on weekdays, and it's free to travel home to avoid the peak hours. People here have the freedom of choosing to handle the business at home first when they receive emails from clients at eight

（自我体会案例：简单重复的工作，没有太大压力，但是对很多人来说也很绝望。最近有个现在公司的同事跟我开玩笑说："Loreen，我觉得我好像这辈子发不了财了，我是一条咸鱼。"本想安慰她，可是想想这貌似是一个事实，她的固定岗位，公司对这个岗位的薪酬预算，已经没有上升空间了。公司也没有新的机会、新的资源给到她，她也无法通过自己在岗位能力的提升，增加更多的收入。反而言之，公司只想花固定的钱，找一个基本能胜任的人即可。这不是个例，很多公司的很多岗位都是这样。）

7. 遇到不合拍的同事，我干得不开心，要不要离开？

想谈这个话题，是我知道有一些同事会因为工作中与同事的一些矛盾而离开，做得不开心，就不想做了。这个是人之常情，很多公司员工离职原因，都有做不开心这一条。可是，可能在每一个环境，每一个公司都有和自己气场不和的人，换哪家都一样。这不仅仅是对于员工，对于领导和老板也是一样，总不可能把那些与自己不合拍的人全部开除吧，工作总还是要做下去的。此处不讲自我调节情绪、改善自我这种观点。客观来说，在CNOOD已经算很好了，大家进来的背景基本都很相

in the morning rather than waiting and shuttling to clock in at the company.

(My experience: Simple and repetitive work does not create much pressure, but it is also desperate for many people. Recently, a colleague at my current company joked to me, "Loreen, I feel that I'm never going to make a fortune in my life. I'm a salted fish—as common as dirt." I tried to comfort her, but on second thought it seemed to be true. The company's budget for her post has peaked. The company cannot provide new opportunities and resources for her. She can't increase her income even by improving her competence at work. Instead, the company just wants to spend a fixed amount of money to find a basically competent person. It isn't a rare case and is true for a lot of positions in many companies.)

7. Shall I leave the company when I'm unhappy to work with colleagues off the beat?

The reason that I discuss this topic is that I know some colleagues choose to leave when they are in conflict with other colleagues at work. If I'm not happy here, I will just leave. This is human nature. Many company employees resign partly because they are unhappy there. However, under every environment, in every company, there might be some people who are at odds with us. It's all the same wherever we go. This is true for employees, leaders and even bosses. It's

似，应届毕业生校招居多，同事年龄也相差不大，大家像同事，更多时候也像同学一样，基本的价值观和做事方法，比较容易协调到一致。而且CNOOD一直也主张，团队自组织，你可以选择和你合拍的人搭档、组队，并不强制分配团队，而且团队也不是固定的。在社招的很多公司，每个人的背景都差异很大，经历也各不相同，有时候要协调一致的观念和做事方法，真的在协调沟通上很费时间，往往只有领导出手，强制分配才能行动。同样，当遇到默契，相互包容支持能同甘共苦的伙伴，真的是一种幸运。在工作一定程度和积累后遇到财富可能不难，更难的是遇到理解吧。老池、佟哥、老虎、Fay、Tina姐、费凤、Ahuan、石头、Neo他们这些合伙人这么久都还没散伙，我想他们是遇到了无条件信任、理解和支持自己的人。

impossible to kick out all the people who are not in tune with the heads. They need people to do the jobs. I'm not talking about the idea of self-regulation or self-improvement. In fact, CNOOD has a relatively good environment: employees have similar backgrounds, as most are recruited directly from college graduates. We are of similar ages, and all colleagues are mostly like schoolmates, with similar basic values and similar ways of doing things. Thus, it's easier for us to reconcile things. Besides, CNOOD has been advocating self-organized teams. You can partner with someone who works in tune with you. Teams are not mandatorily assigned and are also not fixed. In many companies that hire employees by social recruitment, those recruited have quite different backgrounds and experiences. It often takes time to harmonize ideas and ways of work. In most cases the executives have to distribute work. Hence, it's really lucky to meet partners who can understand and tolerate each other and share weal and woe. When we have worked for a period of time with considerable experience, it is not that hard to encounter wealth, While to be understood is much harder. Dennis, Kevin Tong, Tiger, Fay, Tina, Fei Feng, Ahuan, Stone and Neo have been partners for so long and haven't disbanded till now. I think it is because they have met the ones who trust, understand and support each other without conditions.

（自我体会案例：现在创业公司很流

(My experience: The partnership

行合伙人制度，可是合伙人公司还没开始和中途散伙的太多了，公司能够把员工真正当做合伙人那样的去信任，敞开心扉，去分享成果的太少太少，往往败在利益面前，在困难面前。回归到前面提到的，大部分老板开公司的"发心"是给自己赚钱，真正能落实像 CNOOD 这样分配制度的公司鲜有。）

　　夜已深，终于完成了自己心头拖欠两年的一桩心事。不管是现在留在 CNOOD 的家人，还是已经离开的，我想，回过头望，在 CNOOD 的岁月，都将是不负自己的。

　　这封告别信，好像不太"正统"，一般告别信都会写不少感谢某某某，类似的话，反而像在宣讲会的答同学的问。

　　但是我觉得"理解"就是最好的感谢和祝福……
　　大家都多保重，想聚都可以相聚……
　　再见……

附作者和 Dennis 的对话：

Loreen: 老池，交年鉴啦。

Dennis: 非常感谢！看完了，还是您

system is very popular in startups, but there are too many cases where the startups disband halfway. There are very few companies that can earnestly take their staff as partners, trust them, open their hearts and share the benefits together. These companies often lose to benefits and difficulties. As I mentioned before, the "initial purpose" of most bosses to run companies is to make money for themselves. There is barely any company that can share benefits like CNOOD.)

　　It's already late at night, and I've finally taken the load off my mind that has haunted me for two years. Whether those still working at CNOOD or those who have left, I think, as we look back, we will find that we have lived our lives to the full in our days at CNOOD.

　　This farewell letter doesn't seem to be very "orthodox." Generally, a farewell letter would be filled with gratitude to people or similar words, as if answering questions in a lecture.

　　But I think "understanding" is the best gratitude and blessing.

　　Take care, my friends. We can get together whenever we want.

　　See you.

Appendix: WeChat Dialogue with Dennis:

Loreen: Hi, Dennis. Here's my article for the yearbook.

Dennis: Thank you very much! I've

理解我。

Loreen: 早，老池！刚开会去了。

Dennis: 还是您理解我，知道为什么了。

Loreen: 主要是通过这两年接触到的事和人，脑子里好像就自然会理解到为什么CNOOD要这么做。其实在其他几个问题，或多或少，以前我就是理解的。但是在办公室和年鉴这两块，真的是这两年接触才理解。以前我也觉得越商大厦办公室好像一下子费用多了很多，其实可以节约一些的。但是后来发现，每一个人都应该工作和生活得有尊严，都能不被分等级地去对待，在这样环境里的人，长久之后，ta也会给别人尊严。可是现实很多时候没有办法选择自己的生活环境，但是CNOOD想给到大家尽可能好的工作环境。当没有对比，就会把这些忽略。看到很多公司严格的员工等级对待，才理解到您一直倡导的相互尊重。年鉴是因为听一些创业的朋友分享，包括投资人：他们很强调是否要投资一个项目，要看这个项目是否能够产生复利。也就是比如我有一个好的学习方法，我通过抖音发布，可能影响现在成千上万人，和以后未知的人。但是我只在教室分享给1到2个人，影响是极为有限的。

read it out. You are still the one who understands me.

Loreen: Morning, Dennis! I was in a meeting.

Dennis: You understand me and know why I did those things.

Loreen: Through the things and people that I've encountered over the years, it naturally makes me understand why CNOOD operated the way it did. In fact, I understood more or less the issues before, except for the office relocating and the yearbook. I've been acquainted with them and understood them only in recent years. In the past, I thought we spent too much to rent offices in Yueshang Plaza, which I think we should be a little more thrifty. However, later I found out that everyone should work and live with dignity and be treated equally. People working in such an environment for a long period will treat others with dignity. In reality, we most often cannot choose our own living environment, but CNOOD is willing to provide the best possible working environment for its staff. We may ignore it when there is no contrast. Having seen the strict hierarchy of employees in many companies, I've truly understood the mutual respect you have been advocating. My comprehension of the yearbook comes from the inspiration of some startup friends, including investors. When they consider whether to invest in a project, they stress whether the project can produce compound interests. For example, if

Dennis: 学会和公众号、网站，是一个道理。分享出去，知道别人的态度和想法，也知道了自己看不见的东西，从而更好地做下去。

Loreen: 对的。分享即链接，付出即收获。没有主动分享，就不会有交流反馈。

Dennis: 分享是学习。

Loreen: 嗯，是的。是抛出问题，也是自我校正。我看到我现在很多同事完全不愿意去表达自己，主动沟通性很弱。才理解到工作中的人的状态是被公司文化塑造的。这样固化后，很难去改变和接受别人的建议。这也让我理解了，为什么CNOOD要控制社招数量，基本都校招，自己培养。

Dennis: 是的。白纸易画，成图难改。

Loreen: "有温度的企业必定具有宽厚

I have a good learning method, I will release it through Tik Tok to influence thousands of people now and possibly even more people unknown in the future. If I share it in the classroom to only one or two persons, the impact is extremely limited.

Dennis: The CNOOD Society, adopts the same logic as the WeChat account and the website. By sharing we know other people's attitudes and ideas and know things that we cannot see so that we can do even better.

Loreen: That's right. Sharing is linking, and giving is gaining. Without active sharing, there will not be exchanges and feedback.

Dennis: Sharing is learning.

Loreen: Well, yes. By raising questions, we are correcting ourselves as well. I saw that many of my current colleagues are completely unwilling to express themselves and reluctant to take the initiative to communicate. I understand that the state of people at work are shaped by the corporate culture. When people are fixed like this, it is hard for them to make changes and accept other people's advice. I also understand why CNOOD would limit the number of staff recruited from the society and prefer to recruit graduates from universities directly and cultivate them by itself.

Dennis: Yes. It is easier to draw on a piece of white paper and harder to modify a finished picture.

Loreen: "An employee-friendly

仁慈的家国情怀，据此也就一定会有腾空九霄的文化力量。"这是您在公众号发布的文章《父爱》下面的留言。坚持去做，理解的人就会越来越多。

Dennis: 是的，努力加油！

enterprise will surely have a generous and beneficent corporate culture. It will hence have a lofty culture to soar high into the sky." This is a comment to the article "The Paternal Love" that you released in the WeChat official account. Stick to it, and more people will understand you.

Dennis: Yes, let's go for it!

罗 蓉
Loreen Luo

管理学硕士，6年国际商务经验，3年高校大学生辅导员经历，年龄保密。对"人际交往"嗅觉敏锐，喜欢与人打交道，善于并热爱品研"情商管理"理论。通过生活和工作中与人的接触，体会到不论国别和年龄，不论教育与血缘关系，人心都是相通的，只有真心待人，才能获得他人的真心相待。

Loreen, with a master's degree in management, has 6 years' experience of international business and 3 years' experience of being a counselor in a college. Age is a secret. She has an acute sense in interpersonal interactions, love to associate with people, and is fond of as well as good at studying EQ management theories. Through interactions with people in life and at work, she realizes that regardless of nationalities, ages, education backgrounds or blood relationships, people can feel each other's heart and only by treating others with sincerity will one be treated with sincerity by others.

永远一家人

We Are a Family Forever

■ Angela Liu

2013年3月25日，星期一，正式到公司报到，很荣幸成为了施璐德大家庭的一员。

刚进公司那会儿，作为一个新人，心里还是有些忐忑的。不过渐渐地，被公司开放、自由、平等的工作氛围所吸引。公司提倡人人平等，公司领导和同事们和蔼可亲，大家在开放式的办公室工作，也感受不到职级带来的压力。

在这里，公司为每位员工提供一个自我展示的平台，使每个人都能够迅速成长，展现自我。在这里，我们相互关心，相互帮助，创造开心，其乐融融。在这里，只有想不到的，没有做不到的，只要肯努力，勤思考，知难而上，一切都会变为可能。在这里，我找到了自己的归属……

在单证部工作了六年有余，收获满满。感谢公司对我的培养和信任，感谢Dennis的知遇之情。我也很喜欢自己的工作，不忘初心，自己认定的事，就会认

I checked in on March 25, 2013, Monday, to become a member of the CNOOD family.

In the beginning, I, as a newcomer, was a little nervous. Bit by bit, I was attracted by the open, free and equal atmosphere of the work-place. The company advocates equality for all. Everyone is amiable. We work in an open office, without the pressure of job ranks.

The company provides a platform for every member to show ourselves and grow up faster. We care about each other, help each other and create and enjoy infinite happiness. Nothing is impossible here under our fertile imagination. Everything can come true so long as we work hard, think hard and rise to difficulties. I've found my ultimate home in the company.

I have worked in the documentation department for six years and have benefitted a lot from the experience. I am grateful to CNOOD for fostering and

认真真地去做。我喜欢看办公桌上一沓沓堆起的单据，喜欢将它们装订整齐，因为这些都是大家的汗水与努力。我也怀念着在会议室里，跟同事们研究合同、研究标书、研究保险条款的日子，学无止境。我，在这里，和家人们，和兄弟姐妹们一起奋斗，一起努力工作，乐得其所。

trusting me. I am indebted to Dennis for his appreciation. I like my job. I would take seriously what I think I should do. It is pleasant to watch the stacks of documents on my desk, and it makes me even happier to bind them neatly, as they are evidence of our perspiration and efforts. I miss the days in the conference room when I studied contracts, tenders and insurance clauses with my colleagues. Knowledge has no limit. I enjoy working there with all these brothers and sisters, like a family.

都说家家有本难念的经，我家亦如此。闺女从小体质差，身心发展比同龄人都弱一些，所以，孩子的健康成长也是我最大的心愿。2019 年 5 月，我决定要回归家庭，亲自照顾她的衣食住行，给予她更多的陪伴。希望陪伴她的这段时间，她可以慢慢成长，慢慢独立。

跟大家说再见，真是百般不舍。但我相信，无论我在哪里，我们永远都是一家人，我也希望以后有机会，能跟大家再续前缘。

It is said that every family has its own problems. So does mine. My little daughter has suffered from poor health since her childhood. She grows more slowly both physically and mentally than her peers. So my greatest concern is to have her grow up healthily. In May 2019, I decided to go home and take care of her wholeheartedly. I would accompany her she grows up steadily and become independent.

It's hard to say goodbye, but I believe, wherever I am, we will always be a family. I also hope that one day in the future, I can still have a chance to work with you again.

刘 鹤 Angela Liu	1982 年出生，华东师范大学毕业，从事单证工作十余年。 Angela, born in 1982, graduated from East China Normal University and has worked on documents for more than 10 years.

念海霞

For Haixia, My Little Sister

■ Dennis Chi

己亥，端午，凌晨4:26。吾妹，你走了。我们一起，38个春，37个秋，13 899天，333 556小时。你知道的，哥哥非常喜欢你，疼你、爱你、护你。想再牵着你的小手，带你到学校，带你到田野，带你到高山，带你到大海；想再让你骑脖子上，看远方；想再和你一起看课文，追成绩；想再和你一起做早操，锻炼身体……

你从不言语，却最孝。38个春，37个秋，你一直陪伴父母，不离不弃，身体力行，尽力帮扶。有你的日子，妈妈最开心。你和妈妈去田间，和妈妈打猪草，和妈妈去喂牛，和妈妈去拾柴，和妈妈做

It was at 4:26 on the morning of the Dragon Boat Festival of the year 2019 that you, my little sister, departed this life. Together we spent 38 springs and 37 autumns, that is, 13 899 days or 333 556 hours. I, as your elder brother, was fond of you; I cared about you, loved you and always tried my best to protect you—and you knew that. I wish I could once again hold your little hand and take you to the school and the fields, mountains and seas; I wish I could once again carry you on my shoulders and let you enjoy the view in the distance; I wish I could once again read textbooks with you, trying to improve my academic performance; I wish I could once again do morning exercises with you...

You never uttered a word and yet demonstrated the greatest filial piety. You accompanied Father and Mother for 38 springs and 37 autumns and had never abandoned them. You set an example

饭。你吃饭,总是狼吞虎咽,吃得又多又快,像个男孩。妈妈看你吃饭,总是很开心。妈妈做饭当然很好吃,有人欣赏,总是非常赏心悦目的事(小秘密,不要告诉妈妈呀)。有你的地方,妈妈就会安心;有你的笑声,妈妈就会舒展笑容。10年前的这个日子,是爸爸生病的日子。我在想,你们是商量好的吗?爸爸离开的10年里,你一步都没有离开妈妈,陪妈妈哭,伴妈妈笑。你给了妈妈活着的勇气,给了妈妈活着的信心,给了妈妈活好的力量。这人世间,最长情的告白,就是陪伴,最真诚的陪伴。你最孝,哥哥知道,哥哥明白,哥哥记得。

你从不言语,却最爱学。你时常沿着上学的路,一遍遍地走过去,望着上学的学生,看着近在咫尺矗立的学校,听着朗朗的读书声。赶上假期,我归来,你拉着我的手,终于跨过学校的大门,我们昂首走进教室。你开心地笑着,开心地笑着,开心地笑着,手舞足蹈。一会儿,摸摸黑板;一会儿,敲敲课桌;一会儿,坐坐课

for me and did your best to support the family. Mother was the happiest when you were there with her. You kept Mother company when she went to work in the fields, gathered green fodder for pigs, plowed the field with an ox, collected firewood and cooked meals. You always gobbled up all your food like a boy. Mother was always happy to watch you have meals. While Mother is indeed good at cooking, it is always pleasant to be appreciated by others (it's a little secret, don't tell her). Wherever you were, Mother always had peace of mind; wherever your laughter was to be heard, Mother would always laugh heartily too. Father fell ill on the very same day ten years ago. I wonder whether you two had agreed on this. You never left Mother even for an inch during the ten years since Father departed us. You were always with her when she wept or laughed. You gave Mother the courage and confidence to live on as well as the power to live a happy life. In this world, being there with someone, with the most sincerity, is the best expression of love. You have been the most dutiful child—I know, I understand, and I will always remember.

You never uttered a word and yet were the one who loved studying the most. From time to time, you would walk along the road leading to the school, looking at the pupils on their way to school and the campus buildings which stood so near and listening to the pleasant sound of students reading

桌凳；一会儿，有点儿神情落寞。瞅着我，瞅着我，瞅着我。我忽而明白，把随身书籍交给你，让出第一排中间的位置，你静静地坐好，又看着我。我走上讲台，找出几段粉笔，在黑板上写下，"海霞第一课"。你看着我写，听着我读，眼睛亮亮的，闪闪的。你要学习！你想学习！你要学习！你想学习！我分明看懂了你的眼神，读懂了你的心！我和妈妈说，谁知道呢，万一有一天，海霞会说，会写，会读。

　　你从不言语，却执着追求。出生体弱，口不能言，体不能行，你却从没有放弃生命。7岁那年夏天，在学校的我，特别想你，就回家看你。原来你病了！这就是兄妹情谊，这就是六感吧！我抱你起来，学着中医的样子，做推拿。你开始笑，透着坚毅，用眼神告诉我，哥，这没有什么，不要急，不要紧，不要担心。11岁，你刚能蹒跚行走，就学着我的样子，做着运动，数年不停，然后开始跑，开始一步步挑战自己的极限。在一个寒冷冬

books aloud. When I was back home during vacations, you would join hands with me and finally march through the school gate. Holding our heads up high, we walked into a classroom. As happy as a lark, you smiled, thrashing your arms and legs. You touched the blackboard, knocked the desks and sat in the chairs, and then you looked a little lonely. You stared at me. Suddenly I understood what you wanted. I handed my books to you and gave you the middle seat in the front row. You sat there and looked at me silently. I stepped up, stood behind the teacher's desk and found some pieces of chalk. "Lesson One for Haixia" were the words I wrote on the blackboard. When I was writing and reading aloud, you watched me and listened to me attentively. Your bright eyes glittered with eagerness. You wanted to study! You wanted to go to school! Obviously I understood what was in your eyes and your heart. Later I said to Mother, "Maybe one day Haixia will be able to speak, write and read. Who knows?"

　　You never uttered a word and yet showed great perseverance in your pursuit. You had been very frail since you were born. However, you never gave up life even though you could not speak or walk. When you were seven years old, I missed you so much in the summer that I went back from campus to see you. It turned out that you were ill at that time. Maybe this was the tie between a brother and a sister or the "sixth sense." I held

天，你想到远方去看看，一个人走了很远很远，晚上天黑，你找一个地方藏起来，躲避冬天的严寒。还好，妈妈找到了你。我又想起，我把你一个人忘记在漆黑的厨房。我知道你想去远方，去求知，去求学。哥哥知道啊！

妹妹，谢谢你陪伴爸爸、妈妈，谢谢你对哥哥的教诲，教导哥哥要有孝心、要有上进心、要立志做个有用的人。每每想到你，哥哥都惭愧亿分，孝，不如你百万分之一；学，不如你千万分之一；追求，不如你亿万分之一。

妹妹，如有来世，我们还做兄妹，让我疼你，让我爱你，让我维护你。依旧梦

you up and gave you a massage like a traditional Chinese doctor. You began to smile and looked determined. You told me with your eyes, "It's nothing at all. Don't worry!" When you were just able to toddle at the age of eleven, you imitated me and did exercises. You kept on doing exercises for several years before you began jogging. Step by step, you were pushing yourself to the limit. On a chilly winter day, you walked a long way all by yourself because you wanted to go somewhere far away and see a different view. You found a place to hide yourself when it was dark at night, trying to get away from the coldness of the winter. It was lucky that Mother found you soon. I also remember the day when I unintentionally left you alone amid the complete darkness of the kitchen. I know that you always wanted to go somewhere far away to seek knowledge. I know that, my little sister!

My little sister, thank you for having accompanied Father and Mother; thank you for teaching me to be both a dutiful son and a self-motivated man who is determined to contribute to the society. I am extremely ashamed every time I think of you: as a child, you were one million times as dutiful as I am; as a person seeking knowledge, you were ten million times as eager as I am; as a person in pursuit of dreams, you were hundreds of millions times as diligent as I am.

My little sister, let's be brother and sister again and let me love you and

中又遇君，学堂里，追求中。念念来世寻汝处，爱相随，悔无踪。

　　冥冥中，你总在时时警醒我，事事提点我：

　　做人，莫听穿林打叶声，何妨吟啸且徐行，竹杖芒鞋轻胜马，谁怕！一蓑烟雨任平生。

　　做事，料峭春风吹酒醒，微冷，山头斜照却相迎，回首向来萧瑟处，归去，也无风雨也无晴。

　　妹妹，哥哥想你。

protect you if there were indeed a "next life." In a dim dream I saw you again, who was seeking knowledge in the classroom. I could not stop imagining how I will be able to find you in the next life; my love will always be with you, and there will not be regrets any more.

Through a mysterious connection, you have been constantly warning and reminding me:

　　When dealing with other people—
　　Listen not to the rain beating against the trees.
　　I had better walk slowly while chanting at ease.
　　Better than a saddle I like sandals and cane.
　　I'd fain,
　　In a straw cloak, spend my life in mist and rain.
　　When doing my job—
　　Drunken, I am sobered by the vernal wind shrill
　　And rather chill.
　　In front, I see the slanting sun atop the hill;
　　Turning my head, I see the dreary beaten track.
　　Let me go back!
　　Impervious to rain or shine, I'll have my own will.
　　My little sister, I miss you.

池勇海
Dennis Chi

池勇海，男，汉族，1970年生于湖北省仙桃市。武汉理工大学管理学硕士，硕士导师刘国新教授；复旦大学经济学博士，博士生导师洪远朋教授。2008年创立施璐德亚洲有限公司，现担任施璐德亚洲有限公司董事长。

Dennis Chi, male, ethnic Han, was born in Xiantao, Hubei Province in 1970. He received his master's degree in management from Wuhan University of Technology, where he studied under Professor Liu Guoxin, and received his Ph.D. in Economics from Fudan University, where he studied under Professor Hong Yuanpeng. Dennis is now Chairman of CNOOD Asia Limited, which he founded in 2008.

爷 爷

Grandpa

■ Nancy Qi

他半个身子坐躺着　望着窗外	Half lying, he looked out the window,
奄奄一息	At his last gasp.
我一分一秒度过的时间	Every minute and second I spent
是他每时每刻流逝的生命	Was the passing of his life.
他依旧提醒我	He told me as before
穿暖	To keep warm,
吃饱	To eat my fill,
不要给他多花钱	And not to spend money on him.
像极了平日里	It was like a normal day,
只是再也不能	Except he could never again
在门口等我	Wait for me at the door
到车站送我	Or see me off at the station.
他日渐沉重的步伐	His paces became heavy;
慢慢消瘦的身躯	His body became skinny.
他想大声喘气	He wanted to breathe out loud,
却再也使不上力	But was out of steam.
消逝的生命	His life is fading,
和	And
屋里喧哗的人群	The crowd in the room is noisy.
人来　人往	People came and went;
看望他的人络绎不绝	There was a steady stream of visitors.
而谁也	But they all
已然知道结局	Knew the ending,

好无力……
　　此刻
　　泪如雨
2020.3.30

Helpless ...
　At this moment,
　I shed a flood of tears.
2020.3.30

齐晓燕
Nancy Qi

1992年9月出生。是爱挑剔、追求完美的处女座。2014年本科毕业于上海大学材料工程专业，现上海财经大学 MBA 在读。曾在外资企业从事第三方检测。目前是就职于 CNOOD 的第 6 年。愿自己保持快乐，简单，善良。

Born in September 1992, Nancy regards herself as a Virgo who is hypercritical and seeks perfection. She graduated from Shanghai University majoring in materials engineering in 2014 and is currently an MBA candidate at Shanghai University of Finance and Economics. She worked at a foreign company as a third party inspector. This is the sixth year since she joined CNOOD. She hopes that she can keep happy, simple and kind-hearted.

南楼令·中秋

South Tower Song — Mid-Autumn Festival

■ Tony Liu

落叶撒江洲	Over the River oasis are fallen leaves scattered;
疏影映江流	Through her torrents do sparse shadows shine.
十一年重过故楼	Eleven years later am I revisiting the tower.
古栈系舟犹未住	Tied to the ancient sand pier is the boat, and
云邮频叩	Frequent and fast are emails coming via the cloud,
哪里知	Without me knowing
是中秋	That Mid-Autumn Festival is already here.
烟雨游赏处	Amidst the misty rain am I roaming,
谪仙尚在否	Seeking the banished immortal in vain.
旧月明怎添新愁	To the bright old moon are new sorrows added, and
且借吴刚桂花酒	Wu Gang's osmanthus wine have I borrowed.
一饮千秋	Toasting to a thousand autumns am I drinking.
再重头	Starting from scratch again,
少年游	As if still young I'm touring.

注：

自古逢秋悲寂寥，迁客骚人多感时空悲叹，结尾亦曾有"终不似，少年游"的经典。

此曲上阕备陈漂泊流浪感伤之景之情，工作无甲子，岁寒不知年，偶过故地驻足留恋处邮件催发，又哪里知道已是中秋佳节。下阕睹景怀古，旧愁未散平添新愁。但至此行文转折，一饮千秋，思乡，怀旧，悲叹，均已成过眼云烟，一醉过后，毅然前行，不忘初心，再重头，少年游，凭谁问，廉颇老矣，尚能饭否？

Notes:

Since ancient times, people would feel sad and lonely at the arrival of fall. Travelers and poets are particularly sentimental at the seasonal changes. Hence their classic verses often lament their fleeting youth, ending also with missing their "journeys as kids in the good old days."

The first half of the poem narrates the sentimental feelings of an odyssey of life. Having indulged in work for more than a decade, the author happened to revisit the familiar place, stopping and lingering, but was interrupted by countless emails. He was even unaware that it was already the Mid-Autumn Festival. In the second half, the poet cherishes the past at the sight of the scenery, saddened by old and new concerns. Then the tone takes a turn. Drunk to his heart's content, all the homesickness, nostalgia and lamentations are gone like passing clouds. He would forge ahead with resolve, towards the realization of his original aspirations.

别名"观棋柯烂",好古文,寄情于松桂云壑。毕业于上海大学,2016年加入施璐德。

刘 彬
Tony Liu

Tony, also known as "a woodcutter watching the chess game long ago," is fond of Chinese ancient proses and finds enjoyment in natural scenery such as "pine trees, sweet-scented osmanthus and valleys shrouded in clouds." He graduated from Shanghai University and joined CNOOD in 2016.

实习感悟

My Days as an Intern

■ Xuzheng Ren

我本科学习的是环境科学，和公司平时的业务范围相关性不大，所以在公司里学到的东西对我来说都是全新的东西。我学习了怎么看公司的年度财务报表，也去工厂里接触了图纸并进行了分类和标注，平时做得比较多的就是帮忙填写、整理资料。我平时做事情比较快也不太会想到要在做完之后再检查有没有错误，实习期间出现的小纰漏让我意识到在完成任何工作后都要检查一次。在进行文件翻译的时候遇到了一些之前没有接触过的专业内容，在查询词典的同时学到了很多新的词汇，比如一些合同方面的专业词汇，我认为都是对我之后的学习或者工作有帮助的。

有幸听了两次小讲座，第一次讲座让我知道了工作上沟通的重要性，以及就算一开始对某一领域不算精通也可以通过不

I majored in environmental science in college. It had little relevance to CNOOD's regular businesses. So what I learned here were brand new to me. I learned how to read annual financial statements. I went to factories for direct contact with drawings to be classified and labelled. Most of the time, I helped fill in and sort out files. I worked fast but often forgot to check for errors. So I made some small mistakes in the internship. It helped me realize that I should check again once I get a piece of work done. When translating documents, I came across professional contents that I had never met before. I learned many new words while looking them up in dictionaries, such as specialized contract words. I think they will be of some help for my future study and work.

I had the fortune to attend two mini-lectures. The first one taught me the importance of communications at work.

断的努力，边学习边工作。

第二次讲座让我知道了对于项目来说，很多东西都是可以通过沟通来变通的，耐心和冲劲都是必备的，不能被刚开始的小挫折打击得自我后退，可以努力的去磨。就算一开始并没有完全符合业主的要求，比如需要更多的时间来准备，这些都是可以克服的。

之前也在其他公司实习过，可是施璐德给我留下的印象和一般的公司不太一样。施璐德的员工之间的氛围特别融洽，不管做什么都是很团结以及互相帮助的，这和我在学校学到的比较像。我的大学里非常强调团队，很多作业都是需要小组一起完成的，我们都会互相帮助但难免也会有不少分歧，因此我也知道沟通交流真的是一件非常重要的事情。没有工作经验的我其实不太敢发表自己的意见，然后老池告诉了我只要礼数周到就不要惧怕发表自己的意见。

谢谢这次实习让我体会了相较上次实习更完整的实习经历，让我接触了和平时学习的时候不一样的东西，让我走出自己的专业范畴去浅层次地学习一些其他东西，我想这样也能培养我一些更全方面考虑问题的思维。比如，我以后如果从事环境相关的工作，那我可能就也会考虑一下其他人的想法，更高效地和他们交流配合。

It convinced me that even if I was not proficient in a field at first, I could work while learning with constant efforts.

The second lecture allowed me to know that in a project, many things can be solved through communications. In this process, patience and momentum are essential. We shall not be overwhelmed by small setbacks at the start. We should constantly hone ourselves in the process. Even if we didn't meet clients' requirements at first and needed more time for preparation, we can always overcome all the difficulties.

I had worked as an intern in another company before. CNOOD impresses me differently. Its staff are friendly, united and ready to help each other. This is similar to what I learned at school. The universities I attended stress teamwork. It gives assignments to be completed in teams. We help each other, despite our differences. It teaches me that communication is something important. Without any work experience, I did not dare to express my views, but Dennis told me to voice my ideas as long as I'm polite.

I am grateful for this internship as it gives me a more complete experience, enables me to gain access to a new world and learn things beyond the books I studied at school. I think it helps me develop a habit to think in an all-round way. If I take environment-related jobs in the future, I will also consider ideas of people in other jobs and communicate with them more efficiently.

任叙铮
Xuzheng Ren

本科就读于利物浦大学环境科学专业,研究生在伦敦大学学院学习环境系统工程。

Xuzheng Ren received a bachelor's degree in environmental science from Liverpool University and a master's degree in environmental system engineering from University of London.

实习感想

My Internship

■ Leo Jiang

我十分感谢及珍惜在 CNOOD 中的实习经历。在 CNOOD 实习的第一个月中，我跟随 Peter 大哥接触巴拿马项目，了解了整个项目的计划及实施。和他一起去工厂，去设计公司，去幕墙公司的经历开拓了我的眼界。其中我也学到了钢结构的选材和分类，涂漆的分类，如何运输材料，如何联系各个分包商，如何确保整个项目按照时间计划走等，对于整个项目有了多维度的了解。第二个月中，我通过翻译和整理投标文件（不光是巴拿马项目，还有缅甸太阳板项目和曼德勒城市工程项目）学到了招标的流程，也学到了如何为业主做报告。

在公司中，我感受到了"互相关心，创造开心"的公司理念。Peter 总会耐心地回答我的问题，甚至是最基础的问题。在马顿工厂时，Peter 带我参观了每个车

I appreciate and cherish my internship experience at CNOOD. In the first month, I followed Peter to cover the Panama Project. I learned about the plan and the implementation of the project. I followed him to factories, design companies and curtain wall companies to broaden my vision. I also learned how to select and classify steel structures and paints, how to transport materials, how to contact subcontractors and how to ensure that the project go as scheduled. In the second month, I learned about the bidding process and writing the report for the owner by translating and organizing bidding documents (of the Panama project, as well as the Myanmar Solar Panel Project and the Mandalay City Project).

At CNOOD, I have keenly felt the corporate philosophy of "caring for each and creating a new ocean of delightfulness." Peter is so patient to

间以及详细讲解了每个设计流程和工艺，让我学到很多。平时吃饭和同事们聊天也是轻松惬意，完全没有上下级的严肃。

作为一个常年不接触中文的理工男，我并不能写出华丽的语句，对公司只有一句谢谢，感谢池总给我这个机会，感谢前辈们对我的关心，感谢每点学到的知识。

answer my questions, including the most basic ones. In the Matton factory, Peter showed me around in every workshop and explained the processes in details. I learned quite a lot with him. In everyday work, it's relaxing to have lunch together and chat with colleagues without any gap between the superiors and subordinates.

As an engineering student who doesn't have much contact with Chinese texts. I cannot write gorgeous lines. I have only a thank-you to the company. Thank you, Dennis, for giving me this opportunity. Thank you, dear colleagues, for your great loving-care. Thank you, the company, for all the knowledge I have learned here.

蒋励承
Leo Jiang

蒋励承，伊利诺伊大学香槟分校大一学生，系统工程专业。
Leo Jiang is a freshman at University of Illinois at Urbana Champaign, majoring in system engineering.

实习总结

My Internship

■ Shiying Liu

实习期是 2019 年 9 月初至 2019 年 12 月末。通过 4 个月的实习，毫无疑问，我收获很多，成长很多，并且增加了对自己的了解。

首先，在工作能力上。来到这里之后我发现自己是多么的无知（理论和实践侧重点是完全不同的，更何况理论知识并不是很扎实）。在实习过程中通过《UCP600 解读与例证》《ICC 跟单信用证统一惯例》等单证方面的书籍扩大了自己的知识面，更加了解实务中可能出现的情况以及在各方面如何避免出现差错以做到单证相符。在实习期间，我旁听过合同梳理会议，公司项目负责人与工厂负责人有关项目的交谈等，从中学习到了合同的结构，合同所必须涵盖的内容、条款以及交谈的模式、方法等这些在学校大多只是纸上谈兵的部分。在遇到专业知识上的问题时首先要自己查找了解，在了解后或未完全了解时可以请教同事、领导。

I worked at CNOOD as an intern from early September to late December, 2019. In the four months, I learned a lot and grew up a lot and got to knowmyself better.

First, in terms of working abilities, I found how ignorant I was after I came here (anyway, theory and practice have different emphases, not to mention I was yet to consolidate my theoretical studies). During the internship, I read *UCP600 Interpretation and Illustration* and *ICC Uniform Practice for Documentary Credit* to expand my knowledge. Now I have a clearer idea of possible situations in practice and have avoided errors in making documentary credits consistent. In the period, I sat on meetings to sort out contracts and attended project talks with factory managers. I learned about contract structures, contents to be covered in contracts, and modes and methods in conversations, which I had

在实习的过程中，我不断吸收新的知识、建议，以及学习各种技能，并且不断地总结经验、反省，找出自身缺点、分析原因（由于经验不足、能力不够或其他），并且尽可能地加以改正，避免下次再犯。需要努力的是：夯实自己的专业基础，增强对工作的积极性，增强自信心，处事尽力做到不慌乱、不畏首畏尾。

only studied the theories at school. When I encountered professional problems, I tried to find solutions by myself. When necessary, I would consult with colleagues and executives.

In my internship days, I strived to absorb new knowledge, skills and suggestions, sum up experiences and conduct self-examination to find out my own shortcomings and the reasons (lack of experience, poor ability and so on) and correct them to avoid making the same mistakes. It is necessary to consolidate my professional foundation, enhance my enthusiasm for work and my self-confidence and avoid panic and fear in handling matters.

其次,在社交能力上。我在实习之前就了解自己的性格并且想要改变自己,成为一个虽然算不上健谈但在别人的印象里并不是不愿意交流说话的人。但是从这段实习期看来,我并没有完全改变自己——依然是他人眼中不爱说话的人,但至少比之前缩短了变熟络所需的时间。在人多且不熟悉的时候,更愿意聆听、了解或学习,可在周围人看来只是不说话这一事实。改变方式:积极主动和他人交流,不要怕说错话,以提升自己沟通交流的能力。

最后,从学生到初入职场后心理的转变。想让自己的行为、穿着等方面更加规范化,可是起初并不愿改变,导致陷入纠结中。对于初入职场的我来说哪怕可能只是很小、在旁人看起来微不足道的事,都会让我陷入矛盾和自我怀疑中。但是公司

Second, in terms of social competence, I knew myself and wanted to change my personality even before the internship. I wanted to be a person ready for communication, though not necessarily to be talkative. However, it seemed that it didn't work—in the eyes of others, I'm still a person unwilling to talk much. Fortunately, it takes shorter time than before for me to get acquainted with others. In the face of unfamiliar people, I'm more ready to listen and learn. For those around me, I simply don't talk much. In the future, I should take the initiative to talk to others and should not be afraid of saying something wrong to improve my ability to communicate.

Finally, it was a change of mindset from a student to a workplace newbie. I wanted to look more professional in behavior and dressing. In the beginning, I was unwilling to change, which caused me to be entangled. For me, being young and

的氛围和环境出乎意料地好，很幸运初入职场就遇到这么多善良的前辈。

在实习接近尾声的时候，回想 4 个月前的自己，确实成长了许多，不过各方面都还有很大的进步空间。希望以后的自己不要再像之前想法无数，可真实的为之付诸行动的目标却寥寥无几，而是可以更加明确自己的目标并通过不懈的努力完成目标。

以上便是我对于实习期间的总结。愿我们未来皆可期。

inexperienced, a seemingly trivial thing may put me in conflict and cause me to doubt myself. Luckily, the company is wonderful in terms of work atmosphere. I'm grateful to meeting so many kind people at the start of my career.

Now my internship is about to end As I look back, I find I have become more mature than four months ago. Naturally, there is still much room to improve on all fronts. I hope I could bid farewell to my old self who have countless ideas but put few into actions. I will have clearer goals and achieve them with unremitting efforts.

These are what I have learned in the internship. I hope all our dreams come true.

刘诗莹
Shiying Liu

1998 年出生于辽宁鞍山市，就读长春大学旅游学院。实习期为 2019 年 9 月至 2019 年 12 月。

Born in Anshan, Liaoning Province, Shiying Liu is studying at the Tourism College of Changchun University. She interned at CNOOD from September 2019 to December 2019.

实习总结
My Internship in CNOOD

■ Jessie Wang

我的名字叫子樵。我今年18岁,来自福建,现在就读于福建林业职业技术学院。我于7月进入公司,将于8月完成实习。

I am Jessie, 18, from Fujian Province. I am studying at Fujian Forestry Vocational & Technical College. I started my internship at CNOOD in July and will complete it in August.

接下来，我将总结这一时期的工作。

高中毕业后，为了给我一个社会实践的机会，我前往上海，我的姐姐安排我进入 CNOOD 做实习生，尽管我即将开始接触这些陌生的事情，但是我想我能解决这些困难。

在加入 CNOOD 公司之前，我大致了解了 CNOOD，这是一个从事海外国际贸易的公司，我在这认识了很多的哥哥姐姐。我知道 Amir、Billy、Belinde、Danni、Heather、Sherry、Chris Lee 等，他们给了我不同的帮助。所以我非常感谢他们在上海期间对我的帮助。当然，我没有忘记我的姐姐 Fay Lee 和我的老板 Dennis Chi。

虽然这是我的第一次实习，但是我知道服务是一个企业的基础，良好的服务和良好的形象是一个员工的基本准则。所以在实习期间，我穿着整洁，保持着良好的形象。

到了公司的第二天，在姐姐的帮助下，我学会了用公司的软件记录个人名片。虽然花了很长时间，但这对我来说是一个好的开始。

当我开始接手我的第一个任务——完成锂电池的介绍时，我感到紧张和兴奋，并有了一个成功完成它的意愿。有了这样的意愿，我开始我的工作，不断地寻找相关的信息，如锂电池的形成、锂电池市场等，不仅如此，我们也需要知道锂电池行业的工厂和公司情况，而这些需要长时间

The following is a brief summary of my internship at the company.

After graduating from high school, I went to Shanghai to seek a chance of social practice. My elder sister made arrangements for me to work as an intern at CNOOD. Although it was an unfamiliar world, I told myself I could handle all possible difficulties.

Before I stepped into the company, I learned that CNOOD was an international trading company. Here I got acquainted with many elder brothers and sisters, such as Amir, Billy, Belinde, Danni, Heather, Sherry and Chris Lee. They've helped me a lot. I am grateful for their help during my stay in Shanghai. Surely, I will not forget my elder sister Fay Lee and my boss Dennis.

This is my first internship. I know service is the basis of a business, and good service and image are basic norms of an employee. So I dressed neatly to keep a good image.

The second day in the company, my sister helped me to learn how to record personal business cards with the company's software. I spent a long time to command the technique. Anyway, it was a good start for me.

When I was assigned the first task — to brief lithium batteries, I felt a bit nervous and excited. I told myself I would do it perfectly. With this in mind, I went ahead by searching for relevant information such as the formation and the market of lithium batteries. Besides, we also need to

寻找，终于在一个星期后完成了任务。在这个过程中，我发现我学到了很多。

在公司实习期间，我帮助 Danny 去银行盖章或协助 Sherry 上传文件等相对简单的工作。虽然它相对简单，但是它可以丰富我的实习生活，我也学到了很多。我希望在不久的将来，通过我的不断努力，我可以成为其中的一员。

know the producers of lithium batteries. I spent a long time to find them. Finally I completed the task in a week. I found I learned a lot in the process.

In this period, I helped Danny go to the banks for official formalities and assisted Sherry to upload documents to the company's system. They seemed simple but enriched my internship life here. I learned a lot from them. I hope that in the near future, with arduous efforts, I can be a member of this big family.

实习期间，我读完《一个职业经理人的炼金术》，我认为这本书很好。它可以帮助我们处理工作中的一些困难。所以如果你有时间，我想你可以看看这本书。

很高兴能给我这次实习的机会，期待下次与各位见面。

During my internship, I read *The Alchemy of Professional Managers*, a wonderful book. I think it will help us deal with problems at work. So if you have time, read it.

I'm honored to have the opportunity to work as an intern at CNOOD. I look forward to seeing you all next time.

王子樵
Jessie Wang

我的名字叫子樵。我今年 18 岁，来自福建，现在就读于福建林业职业技术学院。

Jessie Wang, 18 years old, came from Fujian Province. He is studying at Fujian Forestry Vocational & Technical College.

图书在版编目(CIP)数据

施璐德年鉴.2019:中英对照/施璐德亚洲有限公司编. —上海:复旦大学出版社,2020.9
ISBN 978-7-309-15169-5

Ⅰ.①施… Ⅱ.①施… Ⅲ.①建筑企业-上海-2019-年鉴-汉、英 Ⅳ.①F426.9-54

中国版本图书馆 CIP 数据核字(2020)第 122993 号

施璐德年鉴.2019
施璐德亚洲有限公司　编
责任编辑/谢同君

复旦大学出版社有限公司出版发行
上海市国权路 579 号　邮编:200433
网址:fupnet@fudanpress.com　http://www.fudanpress.com
门市零售:86-21-65102580　团体订购:86-21-65104505
外埠邮购:86-21-65642846　出版部电话:86-21-65642845
上海丽佳制版印刷有限公司

开本 787×1092　1/16　印张 11.25　字数 253 千
2020 年 9 月第 1 版第 1 次印刷

ISBN 978-7-309-15169-5/F·2714
定价:88.00 元

如有印装质量问题,请向复旦大学出版社有限公司出版部调换。
版权所有　　侵权必究